LEISE SETTINGS OF THE RENAISSANCE AND REFORMATION ERA

RECENT RESEARCHES IN THE MUSIC OF THE RENAISSANCE

James Haar and Howard Mayer Brown, general editors

A-R Editions, Inc., publishes six quarterly series—

Recent Researches in the Music of the Middle Ages and Early Renaissance,
Margaret Bent, general editor;

Recent Researches in the Music of the Renaissance,
James Haar and Howard Mayer Brown, general editors;

Recent Researches in the Music of the Baroque Era,
Robert L. Marshall, general editor;

Recent Researches in the Music of the Classical Era,
Eugene K. Wolf, general editor;

Recent Researches in the Music of the Nineteenth and Early Twentieth Centuries,
Jerald C. Graue, general editor;

Recent Researches in American Music,
H. Wiley Hitchcock, general editor—

which make public music that is being brought to light in the course of current musicological research.

Each volume in the *Recent Researches* is devoted to works by a single composer or to a single genre of composition, chosen because of its potential interest to scholars and performers, and prepared for publication according to the standards that govern the making of all reliable historical editions.

Subscribers to this series, as well as patrons of subscribing institutions, are invited to apply for information about the "Copyright-Sharing Policy" of A-R Editions, Inc., under which the contents of this volume may be reproduced free of charge for study or performance.

Correspondence should be addressed:

A-R EDITIONS, INC.
315 West Gorham Street
Madison, Wisconsin 53703

RECENT RESEARCHES IN THE MUSIC OF THE RENAISSANCE • VOLUME XXXV

LEISE SETTINGS OF THE RENAISSANCE AND REFORMATION ERA

Edited by Johannes Riedel

A-R EDITIONS, INC. • MADISON

To
Heribert Ringmann
and
Günter Bialas

ISSN 0486-123X

ISBN 0-89579-130-7

Library of Congress Cataloging in Publication Data:

Main entry under title:

Leise settings of the Renaissance and Reformation era.
(Recent researches in the music of the Renaissance ; v. 35)
For 3-6 voices; German or Latin words, also printed as text with English translations on p. xxiii.
Includes bibliographical references.
Includes anonymous works and compositions by M. Greiter, J. Heugel, B. Gesius, S. Hemmel, A. Raselius, J. Rasch, B. Hoyoul, L. Daser, C. T. Walliser, H. Braetel, and J. Regnart.
1. Part-songs, Sacred. 2. Part-songs, German. 3. Chorales. I. Riedel, Johannes, writer on music. II. Series.
M2.R2384 vol. 35 [M2082] [M2.3.G47] 780'.903'1s
ISBN 0-89579-130-7 [783.6'75] 80-24343

Contents

Plate I. *Also heilig ist der Tag* from Johann Spangenberg: *Zwölff Christliche Leissen vnd Lobgesenge* (Georg Rhaw: Wittenberg, 1545), pp. 42-43.
The explanatory paragraph on p. 43 is translated as follows:
Interpretation
This is also one of the old Christian *Leisen* and songs of laudation in which the Christian congregation praises our Lord Christ in his holy resurrection.

Preface

The Historico-Liturgical Background

Introduction

A *Leise* is a non-polyphonic folk-hymn that ends with a melodic formula whose text is "kyrie eleison," "kyrio-leis," "kirleis," or "krles."[1] The earliest existing *Leise* that we know of comes from Europe during the Middle Ages.

Leisen were first used for processions. The earliest forerunners of the *Leisen*, the isolated "Kyrie" cries, were used throughout the Middle Ages, particularly during the transportation of a body to a tomb. For example, in the year 819, the fervent disciples of St. Boniface carried his sarcophagus from Mainz to Fulda singing "Kyrie eleison,"[2] and in the year 836, upon the removal of the body of St. Liborius from Mans (France) to Paderborn (Germany), the people sang "Kyrie eleison" while the monks chanted Latin psalms and hymns.[3] *Leise*-like songs were also sung during the processions of the Geissler, a penitential lay-confraternity. In a report of 1349 we find:

> They had the most precious banners of velvet cloth, raw and smooth, and of canopy, the best ones which one might have. They had maybe ten or eight or six banners and maybe as many candles, which people carried in front of them. Wherever they went, to towns or villages, they were greeted with the bells ringing. They followed the banners in couples or in pairs, wearing coats, and two or four of them sang a *Leise*. The *Leise* was:
>
> Nu ist die betevart so her,
> Crist reit selber gen Jerusalem,
> Er vuert ein Kreuze an siner hant:
> Nu helfe uns der heilant:
> Kyrioleis.[4]

Although there are *Leisen* in the Dutch and Czech languages, most are in German, and it is with these German *Leisen* that this edition is concerned. During the Reformation and Counter Reformation some of the medieval "kyrie eleison" formulae (both melodies and texts) were retained. However, some *Leisen* were changed by the substitution of such endings as "Alleluia,"[5] "Alleluia, gelobet sey Gott und Maria,"[6] and "Herr Gott erbarme dich unser."[7] These and many other endings were the result of contemporary Reformation and Counter Reformation needs.[8]

The German *Leisen* repertory consists of the following twelve hymn tunes and the texts that are always associated with them:[9]

Also heilig ist der Tag (1)
Christ ist erstanden (3, 4, 5, 13, 14, 18)
Dys synd die heylgen zehn gebot (2)
Gelobet seistu Jesu Christ (8)
Gott sey gelobet vnd gebenedeiet (7, 10)
In Gottes namen faren wir (17)
Jesus Christus Vnser Heiland, der den Tod überwand (14)
Mensch willst du leben seliglich
Mitten wir im leben sind (6)
Nun bitten wir den heiligen Geist (9, 15)
O du armer Judas
Sei willkommen Herre Christ

The present edition is concerned with the polyphonic Renaissance settings of the *Leisen* texts and tunes in which the *Leise* melody functions as a *cantus firmus*. For example, the settings of "Dys synd die heylgen zehn gebot" (2) and "Gott sey gelobet vnd gebenedeiet" (10) in this edition illustrate a straightforward presentation of the *Leise cantus firmus* in the tenor parts. In both of these settings, the *Leise* tenors present nothing but the *Leise* tune itself; moreover, in order to accentuate the importance of the *Leise* tenor, its entrance is delayed by a number of measures while the other voices initiate their statements. Renaissance polyphonic settings of *Leisen* are typically for four or more voices, and in all of the polyphonic settings of this edition, the melodic material for all voices is derived from the *Leise* tunes. Sometimes, however, this melodic material shows a certain motivic independence from the *cantus firmus*, as may be seen in the initial statement in the bass part of "Gott sey gelobet vnd gebenedeiet" (10).

The *Leise* settings presented in this edition were chosen for the following reasons. (1) To include settings of the *Leisen* that have not been previously published, such as, "Also heilig ist der Tag"[1], "Es giengen drey frauen" [5], "Gott sey gelobet vnd gebenedeiet" [10], "Christus surrexit" [12], "Jesus Christus Vnser Heiland" [14], and "In Gottes namen faren wir" [17]. (2) To include settings that contain simultaneous use of *Leisen* texts and Latin texts (see below). (3) To include compositions by composers whose works are not easily available in modern practical editions, such as Braetel, Daser, Hemmel, Rasch, Raselius, and Regnart. Therefore, together with settings of such relatively well-known *Leisen* as "Christ ist erstanden," this edition also includes typical *cantus firmus* settings of lesser-known *Leise* texts and tunes by lesser-published composers of the Renaissance era. That they are lesser known does not imply that these texts and tunes are of lesser significance or that the lesser-published composers are of secondary importance. It means only that the *Leise* texts and tunes connected with the main church festivals—"Gelobet seistu Jesu Christ" (Christmas), "Christ ist erstanden" (Easter), and "Nun bitten wir den heiligen Geist" (Pentecost)—have been sung more frequently than, for instance, the processional *Leisen* ("Gott sey gelobet vnd gebenedeiet" and "In Gottes namen faren wir") or the didactic *Leisen* ("Dys synd die heylgen zehn gebot" and "Mensch willst du leben seliglich"). The transcription of such lesser-known *Leise* settings in the present edition is intended to fill the gap created by the fact that they are not included in existing historical editions in modern notation. (Such modern transcriptions do include settings of "Mensch willst du leben seliglich," "O du armer Judas," and "Sei willkommen Herre Christ," the three *Leise* texts and tunes not represented in the present edition.)

The General Leise Repertory

As has been stated above, the German *Leise* repertory consists of twelve hymn tunes and their associated texts. The following musical examples give monophonic statements of each melody in the German *Leise* repertory.[10]

The melody of "Also heilig ist der Tag" is:[11]

The melody of "Christ ist erstanden" is:[12]

The melody of "Dys synd die heylgen zehn gebot" is:[13]

The melody of "Gelobet seistu Jesu Christ" is:[14]

The melody of "Gott sey gelobet vnd gebenedeiet" is:[15]

The melody of "In Gottes namen faren wir" is:[16]

The melody of "Jesus Christus, unser Heiland, der den Tod überwand" is:[17]

The melody of "Mensch willst du leben seliglich" is:[18]

The melody of "Mitten wir im leben sind" is:[19]

The melody of "Nun bitten wir den heiligen Geist" is:[20]

The melody of "O du armer Judas" is:[21]

The melody of "Sei willkommen Herre Christ" is:[22]

The above melodies are distinguished by musical qualities that pertain to the entire medieval and Renaissance repertoire of "songs of laudations"[23] (i.e., the *Leisen*) and chorales. These qualities include pentatonicism, modality, bar form, and other melodic aspects that will be discussed below.

PENTATONICISM

Some *Leise* tunes have specific pentatonic qualities. Such qualities result when a melody uses very few or no half-tones. For instance, the monophonic example of "Nun bitten wir den heiligen Geist" (see above) shows a half-tone progression (e' to f') only in the final "Kyrieleis." Moreover, the use of a succession of a major and minor third (g'-b'-d'') in this *Leise* gives it a pronounced "pentatonic" flavor.

"Nun bitten wir" is not the only *Leise* to show pentatonic qualities. The melody of the first phrase of "Christ ist erstanden" is characterized by the absence of the half-tone progression b′ to c″.

Modes

All of these *Leise* melodies, whether they show pentatonic features or not, can be classified within the ecclesiastical mode system.[24] "Christ ist erstanden" is in the Dorian mode. "Also heilig ist der Tag," "Mensch willst du leben seliglich," and "Mitten wir im leben sind" are in the Phrygian mode. "Dys synd die heylgen zehn gebot," "Gelobet seistu Jesu Christ," "In Gottes namen faren wir," and "O du armer Judas" are all in Mixolydian, while "Gott sei gelobet vnd gebenedeiet" is in Hypomixolydian. "Jesus Christus, unser Heiland, der den Tod überwand"[25] is in the Aeolian (minor) mode, and "Nun bitten wir den heiligen Geist" and "Sei willkommen Herre Christ"[26] are in the Ionian (major) mode.

The Bar Form

As in the majority of the "songs of laudations" and chorales, the *Leise* tunes show the use of different types of musical structures. Many of these structures resemble the bar form, which is based on a principle of repetition and contrast. In its simplest manifestation, the bar form consists of two musical phrases and their repetition (known as the *Stollen*) and a concluding, contrasting section called the *Abgesang*.[27]

There are three different types of bar forms:

	Stollen	*Abgesang*
Repetition bar form	:a-b:	c a b
Serial bar form	:a-b:	c d e
Repetition serial bar form	:a-b:	c d a b

Only three of the *Leisen* use the bar form proper, and when they do, it is the Repetition serial bar form. These *Leisen* are "Gott sey gelobet vnd gebenedeiet" (with the scheme :a b: c a d e c), "Mitten wir im leben sind" (with the scheme :a b: c d b e e a f a b g), and "Christ lag in Todesbanden" (:ab: c a′d b′).

"Also heilig ist der Tag" shows characteristics of the Serial bar form, but the *Stollen* (a b) is not repeated literally. Its scheme is a b a′ b′ b″ a″ c d. "Jesus Christus Vnser Heiland, der den Tod überwand" is also in a form that closely resembles bar form, but the *Abgesang* is placed between the two *Stollen* statements in this *Leise* rather than after them. Its scheme is a a b c a b.

Serial organization that does not make use of the *Abgesang* of the bar form seems to be a favorite compositional procedure in *Leise* tunes. Thus, a b b′ c d is the scheme of both "Dys synd die heylgen zehn gebot" and "In Gottes namen faren wir." "Mensch willst du leben seliglich," "Nun bitten wir den heiligen Geist," and "Sei willkommen Herre Christ" have a scheme (a b c d e) that is almost identical to that of "Dys synd die heylgen zehn gebot," and "In Gottes namen faren wir." The *Leise* "O du armer Judas" is almost monomotivic in that the a-phrase is presented in four different ways. The scheme is: a b a′ c a″ d a‴ b e e′ a⁗.

Specific Melodic Qualities

As in the majority of the repertoire of the chorales, a repeated tone-pattern occurs at the beginning of some of the *Leisen*. For example, the melodies of "Dys synd die heylgen zehn gebot," "Gelobet seistu Jesu Christ," "Gott sey gelobet vnd gebenedeiet," "Jesus Christus Vnser Heiland, der den Tod überwand," and "O du armer Judas" begin with from three to six statements of the same tone-pattern.

"Dys synd die heylgen zehn gebot," "In Gottes namen faren wir," and "Gelobet seistu Jesu Christ" show the beat of the first tone shortened by half.[28] The time value of the first tone of "Gott sey gelobet vnd gebenedeiet," however, is doubled. The doubling of the time value of the first tone also occurs in "Christ ist erstanden," "Mensch willst du leben seliglich" and "Nun bitten wir den heiligen Geist."[29]

Leisen Associated with "Christ ist erstanden"

Five other closely related pre-Reformation *Leisen* are associated with "Christ ist erstanden." They form the following group:[30]

Christ der ist erstanden
Christ lag in Todesbanden (11, 16)
Christus surrexit mala nostra texit (3, 12)
Surrexit Christus hodie/Erstanden ist der heilig Christ
Christ fuhr gen Himmel

The various tunes of the "Christ ist erstanden" sub-group are as follows.

"Christ der ist erstanden":[31]

"Christ der ist erstanden" has a melody that, although it has remnants of the "Christ ist erstanden" melody, is largely a separate tune. Johannes Rasch's four-part settings (no. 9 through no. 13 in his *Cantivncvlae Paschales*) make use of the "Christ ist erstanden" melody.[32]

"Christ lag in Todesbanden":[33]

"Christus surrexit mala nostra texit" is the same as the melody of "Christ ist erstanden" (see above, p. viii for this melody).

The melody of "Surrexit Christus hodie/ Erstanden ist der heilig Christ" differs from the melody of "Christ ist erstanden." However, the "Surrexit Christus hodie/Erstanden ist der heilig Christ" *Leise* is included in the "Christ ist erstanden" subgroup because it is related to that group textually (see below). The "Surrexit/Erstanden" melody is as follows:[34]

"Christ fuhr gen Himmel":[35]

Again, as in the case of the general *Leise* repertoire, certain musical and textual qualities exhibited by the *Leisen* associated with "Christ ist erstanden" will be discussed below.

Pentatonicism in the Leisen of the Subgroup—In "Christ der ist erstanden," the pentatonic quality is stressed by a predominance of major- and minor-third progressions. However, in "Christ lag in Todesbanden," half-steps have filled out the pentatonic gaps of the original "Christ ist erstanden" melody, and the resulting tune is actually more similar to the sequence "Victimae paschali laudes" (see below for a discussion of the relationship of *Leisen* to sequences). Since "Christ fuhr gen Himmel" and "Christus surrexit mala nostra texit" are musical replicas of "Christ ist erstanden," the latter's pentatonic quality prevails in both of them.

Modes in the Leisen of the Subgroup—"Christ der ist erstanden," "Christ lag in Todesbanden," "Christus surrexit mala nostra texit," and "Christ fuhr gen Himmel" are in the Dorian mode. "Surrexit Christus hodie/Erstanden ist der heilig Christ" is in the Ionian (major) mode.

The Bar form in the Leisen of the Subgroup—In contrast to "Christ ist erstanden," "Christ lag in Todesbanden" shows a Repetition serial bar form of :a b: c d e b. (The second half of d has the same melody as the second half of a, and e is related to b. Only the second half of b is used for the final statement.) "Christ fuhr gen Himmel" and "Christus surrexit mala nostra texit," like the original "Christ ist erstanden," employ a scheme of a b c b d. "Christ der ist erstanden," and "Surrexit Christus hodie/ Erstanden ist der heilig Christ" show a serial organization that does not make use of the *Abgesang* of the bar form.

Textual considerations in the Leisen of the Subgroup—The most distinguished place within the "Christ ist erstanden" group is held by Luther's "Der Lobsanck Christ ist erstanden gebessert," the title he gave to a melody that carried the text "Christ lag in Todesbanden."[36] Luther's "gebessert" version of "Christ ist erstanden" ("Christ lag in Todesbanden") is well represented among the "Christ lag in Todesbanden" settings by Renaissance and Reformation era composers.[37]

Luther's revised enlargement of the "Christ ist erstanden" text uses the word "Todesbanden," which was sung centuries before in connection with "Christ ist erstanden." Another example of an early use of this word occurs in a song attributed to Konrad von Queinfurt (1382), a stanza of which includes

> ...nun singet: Christus ist erstanden wol hiute von des todes banden.[38]

The first line of text in all three "Christ ist erstanden" settings in the *Glogauer Liederbuch* (probably written between 1477 and 1488) reads: "Christ [der] ist erstanden von des Todesbanden."[39] Use of the "Todesbanden" text with the "Christ ist erstanden" melody persisted in the seventeenth century. The third melody (Discantus, Altus, Bassus primus) of the "Christ ist erstanden" appears in the *Andernach Gesangbuch*, 1608, with the text:

Christus ist erstanden,
Kyrie eleison
von des Todesbanden,
Alleluia,
gelobt sey Gott und Maria.[40]

The number of "Christ lag in Todesbanden" settings is increased still more in the baroque era, with Michael Praetorious's and Johann Sebastian Bach's settings being the most outstanding examples of baroque *Leise* literature.[41]

The next most frequently set text after "Christ lag in Todesbanden" is the "Surrexit Christus hodie / Erstanden ist der heilig Christ." Although the "Surrexit/Erstanden" tune has no melodic similarities to the "Christ ist erstanden" melody, textual interpolations of the "Christ ist erstanden" text within the "Surrexit/Erstanden" versifications place it within the "Christ ist erstanden" group. For example, Johannes Leisentritt's version of the "Erstanden ist der heilig Christ" text contains, in its second, third, and fourteenth stanzas, direct quotations from the second and third stanzas of the original "Christ ist erstanden" text.[42] In Michael Praetorious's three-part setting of the "Erstanden ist der heilig Christ," four stanzas of text are from "Erstanden ist der heilig Christ," and four others are from "Christ ist erstanden."[43]

A further example of insertion of the "Surrexit/ Erstanden" text occurs in a "Christ ist erstanden" *Leise* from St. Gall (1540), whose third stanza is comprised of the "Surrexit" text.[44] The "Christ ist erstanden" version of the *Koeln Gesangbuch* (1600) also has the "Surrexit" text in its third stanza.[45] The interchangeability of these two texts is shown in a manuscript from 1478 in which the Latin version of the "Surrexit" alternates with the vernacular "Christ ist erstanden."[46] Such insertions of the "Surrexit/Erstanden" text within the "Christ ist erstanden" reassert Hoffmann's thesis regarding the historical coexistence of the "Surrexit/Erstanden" and "Christ ist erstanden" tunes.[47]

The "Surrexit" text is not the only one that is occasionally associated with the "Christ ist erstanden" text. Both in the above example from Leisentritt and in a tenor part book from Eisleben (1598),[48] the nineteen stanzas of the "Erstanden ist der heilig Christ" setting contain the "Christ ist erstanden" text and melody as well as the text and melody of the *Leise* of the three Marys, "Es giengen drey frauen."[49] Another outstanding musical example of the insertion of the "three Marys" *Leise* within a "Christ ist erstanden" setting is no. 5 of this edition (see Critical Notes for sources).

Sometimes polyphonic settings of "Christ ist erstanden" or other *Leisen* occur in which some of the voice-lines carry a Latin text, while others simultaneously carry a German text. A most interesting example of such simultaneous text-usage occurs in the anonymous six-part setting (no. 14 in the present edition) of "Jesus Christus vero est agnus–Jesus Christus Vnser Heiland/Gratia sit Deo–Christ ist erstanden."[50]

Leise Usage

Long before the Reformation era, *Leisen* were incorporated into liturgies for the Christmas, Lent, Easter, and Pentecost seasons of the Church year. *Leisen* were used both in Roman Catholic and, after the Reformation, in Lutheran churches. Moreover, many *Leisen* were sung at sacred events not connected with the formal Sunday liturgies; for example, there are *Leisen* for pilgrimages, processions, burial services, and for church-related teaching purposes.

Leisen in the Roman Catholic Church

Within the liturgy of the Roman Church, the position of the *Leise* was generally the same as that of any other sacred vernacular song. German songs were permitted at the following places in the liturgy: (1) before the beginning of the service;[51] (2) as an interpolation of a sequence [gradual];[52] (3) at the sermon;[53] (4) at the Elevation;[54] (5) at the end of the service.[55]

Moreover, as early as the close of the twelfth century, specific liturgical recommendations were given for the singing of the Christmas *Leise* "Sei willkommen Herre Christ" at the close of Matins and immediately preceeding the "Te Deum laudamus."[56] A Roman Church order of 1519 specifies the singing of the Christmas *Leise* "Gelobet seistu Jesu Christ" by the congregation; according to the order, this *Leise* was preceded by a choral performance of the Christmas sequence "Grates nunc omnes."[57]

Liturgical recommendations concerning the use of the *Leisen* were applied also to other Roman Church festivals. The Lenten *Leise* "O du armer Judas" was used for Matins during Holy Week.[58] The Easter *Leise* "Christ ist erstanden"[59] was sung immediately preceeding the "Te Deum Laudamus" at the Easter Eve (vigil) service.[60] A Roman Catholic Church order of 1491 recommends that on Sundays from Easter to Pentecost the congregation sing the

Leise "Nun bitten wir den heiligen Geist" before and after the sermon.[61]

LEISEN IN THE LUTHERAN CHURCH

In the Lutheran Mass, *Leisen* were often sung during or after the Communion service. Favorites for this point in the Mass were: "Gott sey gelobet vnd gebenedeiet";[62] "Nun bitten wir den heiligen Geist";[63] and "Jesus Christus Vnser Heiland, der den Tod überwand."[64] "Nun bitten wir den heiligen Geist" was also often sung after the reading of the Epistle. During the course of the sixteenth and seventeenth centuries, however, "Nun bitten wir den heiligen Geist" was customarily sung after the sermon in many Lutheran churches. Other favorite post-sermon *Leisen* in the Reformation and post-Reformation eras were "Mitten wir im leben sind" and "Dys synd die heylgen zehn gebot."

As in the Roman Catholic Church, *Leisen* were often sung in the Lutheran liturgy to mark the seasons of Christmas, Lent, Easter, and Pentecost during the Church year. For example, the Christmas *Leise* "Gelobet seistu Jesu Christ" was sung in both Lutheran and Roman Catholic churches. This is also true for the Lenten, Easter, and Pentecost *Leisen*. "Jesus Christus Vnser Heiland, der den Tod überwand" was sung at Easter in both churches, and both shared in singing "Nun bitten wir den heiligen Geist" at Pentecost.

NON-LITURGICAL LEISEN

Just as there were certain *Leisen* appropriate to non-liturgical, but church-related, events in the Roman church, so also were there non-liturgical *Leisen* in the Lutheran church. Many of these *Leisen* were associated with the same events in both churches. These events and their associated *Leisen* are as follows: processions ("Gott sey gelobet vnd gebenedeiet"); pilgrimages ("In Gottes namen faren wir"); burial ("Mitten wir im leben sind"); didactic[65] [based on Ten Commandments] ("Mensch willst du leben seliglich" and "Dys synd die heylgen zehn gebot"); and liturgical plays ("Christ ist erstanden").[66]

LEISEN IN RELATION TO LITANIES, KYRIES OF MASSES, AND SEQUENCES

The monophonic *Leisen* draw their motivic material for the cadential "Kyrie eleison" formulae from litanies rather than from the "Kyrie" of the Mass. The All Saints litany is the source of motivic material for the majority of the "Kyrie" types appearing in the last measures of those *Leisen* that were put into notation between the fourteenth and eighteenth centuries. The Loreto, St. Joseph, and Sacred Heart litanies and the "Preces" are also important motivic sources used in the creation of the *Leise* cry. However, when these monophonic *Leisen* provide *canti firmi* for polyphonic settings, the influence of the surrounding voices in these settings causes the traditional *Leise* melodies to lose some of their original motivic characteristics. Under this influence, then, these *Leise canti firmi* show characteristics of the Kyries of various Masses.[67] These source Kyries occur in the following Masses: *Missa Clemens Rector; Missa Splendor Aeterne; Missa Te Christe Rex Supplices; Missa Firmator Sancte; Missa Cum Jubilo; Missa Dominator Deus; Missa Lux et Origo; Missa Stellifesu Conditor Orbis; Missa Jesu Redemptor; Missa Altissime*.

Other *Leisen* are melodic variants of certain Gregorian sequences. In the following list, the title of the original Latin sequence is given, followed by the title of the *Leise* derived from that sequence:[68] Victimae paschali laudes ("Christ ist erstanden"); Veni sancte spiritus ("Nun bitten wir den heiligen Geist"); Grates nunc omnes ("Gelobet seistu Jesu Christ"); Jesse virgam humidavit ("Sei willkommen Herre Christ"). In fact, these *Leisen* were sometimes sung in conjunction with their "parent" sequences. For example, at the end of the twelfth century the *Leise* "Christ ist erstanden" was often sung immediately following the sequence "Victimae paschali laudes" in the liturgical play *Visitatio sepulchri*.[69] Sequences and their derivative *Leisen* are in close proximity in some of the polyphonic settings of the Mass, as well. For example, in the *Glogauer Liederbuch* of the fifteenth century, a polyphonic rendition of the "Victimae paschali laudes" is followed immediately by a three-voice setting of "Christ ist erstanden."[70] The Protestant *Kirchenordnung* of Brandenburg-Nuremberg, 1533, suggests the successive singing of "Victimae paschali laudes" and Luther's revised version of "Christ ist erstanden" (i.e., "Christ lag in Todesbanden").[71]

An Easter Mass, "Prosa de Resurrectione" by Johannes Galliculus (Hehnel), published by Georg Rhaw in 1539 in his *Officia paschalia*, provides an example of the simultaneous singing of the text and tune of a *Leise* together with its "parent" sequence;[72] in this example, three melodic phrases from the "Victimae paschali laudes" sequence are combined with a phrase from the "Christ ist erstanden" *Leise*. An example of a simultaneous combination of a *Leise* with one of the variants derived from it is Max Greiter's motet (no. 3 in the present edition) in which "Christ ist erstanden" is joined with "Christus surrexit." "Christus surrexit" is one of the five *Leisen* in the subgroup derived from "Christ ist erstanden."[73]

Some Individual Settings

The selection of individual polyphonic *Leise* settings contained in this edition covers a time span of 225 years, from an early Renaissance three-voice composition, "Also heilig ist der Tag," ca. 1400 (no. 1), to an early baroque five-voice setting of "Christ lag in Todesbanden" (no. 16) by Christoph Thomas Walliser (1625). The majority of settings in this edition demonstrates a chronological stylistic development illustrated by non-imitative, canonic, through-imitative, and concerted writing. However, some of the settings, such as nos. 2, 5, 6, 8, 10, 11, 15, 16, and 17, do not offer any further illustrations of such stylistic changes; thus, these settings are not discussed below.

Also heilig ist der Tag

The three-voice settings of the Easter *Leise* "Also heilig ist der Tag" (no. 1) has the *cantus firmus* (i.e., the *Leise* melody) in the Tenor. In this work, the Tenor is the middle voice, and it has the range of a contra-tenor altus, going from g to g'; the Discant range is d' to d"; and the Contra-tenor range in this work is from d to g. A crossing of voices between the Tenor and the Contra-tenor occurs toward the end of certain phrases in this work.

In the source, the entire setting is presented without any rests; the *caesurae* between each of the phrases are indicated by a semibrevis for the corresponding *finalis*. No hint of any imitation exists. The semibrevis values indicating *caesurae* always appear in the *cantus firmus*; semibreves sometimes occur in the other two voices as well. When the other two voices are not singing semibreves at *caesurae*, they sing ornamental figures while the *cantus firmus* note is held. Such ornamental figures can be classified as belonging to three different types: (1) the Kyklosis (Circulatio), a figure of circulatory motion; (2) the Anabasis (Ascensio), a figure of ascending motion; (3) and the Katabasis (Descensus), a figure of descending motion. Some relationship exists between these figures and the text; for example, all three figures occur in the outer voices at the words "Teufel darinnen fand" to portray the idea of the resurrection of Christ. The Tenor *cantus firmus*, however, stands apart without embellishment. The Contra-tenor generally moves in contrary motion to the Tenor, while the Discant is primarily an accompanying voice.

Christ ist erstanden/Christus surrexit

The Max Greiter setting (no. 3) simultaneously employs two different but related texts ("Christ ist erstanden" and "Christus surrexit"), both of which are set to the *cantus firmus* melody of the "Christ ist erstanden" *Leise*. The Cantus part carries the German "Christ ist erstanden" text, while the three other voices carry the Latin "Christus surrexit mala nostra texit" text (see Texts and Translations, p. xxiii): the Altus and Bassus present the Latin text without interruption; however, the Tenor (labelled "Vagans" in the source) makes a momentary departure from the Latin text, as it has a "fro sein" after the "et quos hoc dilexit" statement. All voices are nourished by the same *cantus firmus* material, which appears in its purest form in the Cantus part. The first and fourth phrases of the *Leise* tune are given twice in the Cantus; in its second presentation, the first phrase is transposed up a fourth. Many melodic insertions and extensions occur in all voices; and even in the Cantus part there are occasional *fiorituras* (e.g., at the word "fro"). Continuous imitative writing using *cantus firmus* materials emphasizes the importance of the Cantus and the Tenor parts in this piece. Near the end of the setting, Greiter sets these same two voices in canonic relationship in order to carry the important words: "Christ sol vnser trost sein" (in the Cantus) and "nos ad coelos vexit" (in the other three voices). The final plagal cadence is embellished with a melismatic figure.

Christ ist erstanden

Joan Heugel's setting of "Christ ist erstanden" (no. 4) was written for six voices in 1541. The piece presents an interesting contrast within itself in that the two voices (Cantus II and Bassus) use the *Leise* material freely, while the other four voices give fairly strict renditions of the *Leise* melody. For instance, during the realization of the very first phrase, the Cantus II has a countermelody that is opposed to the phrase material of the Tenor *cantus firmus* and the Cantus I part, both of which are quite straightforward in their presentation of the *Leise* material. With the exception of the first phrase, the Tenor part states each phrase of the *Leise* twice; however, the second statement is often slightly varied. All statements are separated in true tenor-*lied* fashion by long rests. The tenor-*lied* façade of this setting is considerably strengthened by the fact that the Altus I carries the *cantus firmus Leise* without any embellishment and stands in a quasi-canonic relationship to the *cantus firmus* in the Tenor. As in the Cantus II part, the melodic lines of the Altus II part flow with few interruptions throughout the entire setting. The motivic materials of the Altus II part are taken from the *Leise* tune and from its melodic and rhythmic expansions. Throughout Heugel's set-

ting, both motive-bound and independent melodic elements intermingle in the secondary voices to provide contrast with the paired *cantus firmus* statements in the Altus I and Tenor parts. By dividing the Cantus I and Bassus parts in the final measures of the piece, Heugel achieves a fuller sound in the final measure of the work.

Gott sey gelobet vnd gebenedeiet

The four-voice setting of "Gott sey gelobet vnd gebenedeiet" (no. 7) by Sigmund Hemmel is a typical altus-*lied* composition. The entire piece revolves around the Altus, which alone presents the *cantus firmus* without any major alterations. The other voices incorporate the *Leise* material only occasionally, and they seem to be mere by-products of the *cantus firmus* presentation. All complex and sophisticated imitative networks of polyphony are abandoned in favor of the simpler "Binnen" harmonization (chordal filling-out by the inner voice) of root chords on I, IV, I at the beginning. Moreover, the "typecast" progressions of the Bassus that stress the intervals of the fifth and the octave and the occasional use of "Schein" polyphony-homophony, wherein even the polyphony that does exist is dominated by a homophonic feeling, both contribute to the clarity of the setting of the *cantus firmus*.

Nun bitten wir den heiligen Geist

Johannes Rasch's five-voice setting of "Nun bitten wir den heiligen Geist" (no. 9) illustrates this composer's typical placement of the *cantus firmus* in the Bassus voice. A great deal of imitative action occurs in this piece, with the Bassus and the Cantus showing the strongest imitative interdependence. Although the Cantus part imitates the first phrase of the *Leise* almost literally, this part goes on to state only the antecedent of the second phrase (transposed by a fifth), and it imitates only the head motive of the third phrase. The Altus and Tenor I parts very freely anticipate some of the *cantus firmus* material, and of all the inner voices, the Tenor II has the least dependence on the *cantus firmus*.

With the exception of the Bassus, all parts make use of small note values throughout the setting. The predominance of small note values, the location of the *cantus firmus* in only the lowest part, and the fact that text underlay is found only in the Bassus part of the source manuscript all lead the present editor to recommend an instrumental rendition of this piece.

Christus surrexit and Christ ist erstanden

Certain features of "Christus surrexit" (no. 12) and "Christ ist erstanden" (no. 13) suggest that these two settings could be performed successively. Both are in six voices, both stress the through-imitation style of writing, and both share the same *cantus firmus* melody.

Canon-like procedures permeate "Christus surrexit," particularly between the Tenor and Bassus I (labelled in the source as Vagans) parts. Imitation begins in this setting as the Altus presents the first phrase of the *Leise* tune, and as each of the imitating voices (Tenor, Bassus I, Bassus II) enters successively after the passage of one and one-half measures. The "Kyrie eleison" finale is distinguished by the sudden appearance of shorter note values.

In "Christ ist erstanden" (no. 13), countersubjects move against the *cantus firmus*. This type of movement can best be seen in the first seven measures, where the Cantus I, Altus, and Bassus carry countersubjects against the Tenor *cantus firmus*. The prominence of the countersubject of the Cantus I is further emphasized by the fact that the Cantus II repeats this subject after a delay of three measures.

Jesus Christus vero est agnus–
Jesus Christus Vnser Heiland/
Gratia sit Deo–Christ ist erstanden

In the anonymous bi-sectional motet "Jesus Christus vero est agnus–Jesus Christus Vnser Heiland/Gratia sit Deo–Christ ist erstanden" (no. 14), two texts—one in German and the other in Latin—are sung simultaneously in the first section (mm. 1-75). The Cantus II carries the German text, while the other five voices carry the Latin text. In this first section, the "Jesus Christus Vnser Heiland" melody and text are given only in the Cantus II part, which, after stating the first three phrases of German text without interruption, briefly joins the other five voices in stating the second phrase of the Latin text of "Jesus Christus vero est agnus"; the Cantus II part then returns to the presentation of the fourth and final phrase of the "Jesus Christus Vnser Heiland" *Leise*.

Two other texts are sung simultaneously in the second section of this motet. Here, the Altus carries the German text ("Christ ist erstanden"), while the remaining voices carry the Latin "Gratia sit Deo." The "Christ ist erstanden" melody and text is stated only in the Altus, where it is presented in long note values with phrases separated from each other by long rests. The remaining voices, carrying texts that deal with praise and victory, are occupied with through-imitative statements that do not exploit the *cantus firmus* motivic material. Rather, once the *Leise* text has been completely stated, the *cantus firmus* voice (the Altus) joins the final "per Jesum Christum" exclamations of the remaining five voices. As in the first section of this composition, the straightforward statements of the *Leise* melody contrast sharply with the highly embellished elaboration of its Latin counterpart.

Regnart's Missa IV: Christ ist erstanden

Jacob Regnart's *Missa IV: Christ ist erstanden* (no. 18) is unique among Masses in that the entire composition, except for the "Et iterum venturus est," is based on motivic material from the melody of this Easter *Leise*. One other polyphonic Mass, written by Johannes Galliculus (Hehnel) and printed by Johannes Rhaw in 1539, does include *cantus firmus* material from the "Christ ist erstanden" *Leise*;[74] however, this Mass is not completely dependent on the *Leise* melody, as Regnart's work is. Composed in 1599, Regnart's *Missa IV* is written for five voices. This work is combined with eight other polyphonic Masses for five, six, and eight voices in a collection entitled *Missae ad imitationem selectissimarum cantionarum*, printed in Frankfurt in 1602, after Regnart's death.[75] The dedication of the *Missae ad imitationem selectissimarum cantionarum* seems to indicate that Regnart was aware that he was near the end of his life as he composed his *Missa IV*. A translation of this dedication follows:

> Alas! I am forsaken of men. My body languishes; sudden infirmity seizes me. I am driven to seek the covers of my [death] bed. My faculties presage an enormous future calamity. Either I am brought to my end quickly by death, or my ruin is completed with the peril to my life sustained for a long time. Unless I am mistaken, the time of my languor will even now draw nigh! I see that nothing is to be changed. This my meanest hand ought to set to these my greatest works: enough to have sung 'til now; enough to have composed songs; enough to have lived in good taste.[76]

Regnart's Mass freely follows the form of the Ordinary of the Roman Catholic Mass. The Credo of *Missa IV* consists of five independent parts: (1) "Patrem, factorem coeli et terra"; (2) "Et incarnatus est"; (3) "Crucifixus etiam"; (4) "Et iterum venturus est"; and (5) "Et in spiritum sanctum." This composition shows complete command of the mannerist style typical of Regnart's time. The composer handles the *Leise* material with utmost grace, elegance, and control.

Treatment of the Leise material in Regnart's Missa IV

Regnart has used the "Christ ist erstanden" melody as a *cantus firmus* throughout Missa IV; however, the phrases of the original *Leise* melody are usually altered slightly to suit the composer. Only two of the *Leise* phrases (the first and the third) are quoted literally in this Mass. Literal quotations of the first *Leise* phrase occur four times, all in the first "Kyrie eleison." The third *Leise* phrase is quoted literally in the second "Kyrie eleison" (twice) and in the "Qui tollis peccata mundi" (twice).

The Regnart Mass presents the four phrases of the *Leise* melody in the following way. The Kyrie presents one complete statement of the *Leise*: the first "Kyrie eleison" carries phrase 1; the "Christe eleison" is based on phrases 2 and 3; and the final "Kyrie eleison" quotes the third *Leise* phrase literally and also contains melodic material from phrase 4 and the Alleluia. The Gloria is based on one complete statement of the entire *Leise* melody. Four of the five sections of the Credo, use *Leise* material: (1) the "Patrem factorem" presents phrases 1 and 2 and the Alleluia; (2) the "Et incarnatus est" carries phrase 1; (3) the "Crucifixus etiam" is based on phrases 2, 3, 4, and the Alleluia; and (4) the "Et in spiritum sanctum" presents the entire *Leise* model. Only the "Et iterum venturus est" section of the Credo is without *Leise* material. The Sanctus carries one statement of the *Leise* minus the Alleluia; the Benedictus is based on phrases 1 and 3 and on the Alleluia; and the Agnus Dei, like the Sanctus, makes use of one *Leise* statement without the Alleluia.

The *cantus firmus* material, whether it is a statement of the original *Leise* or an altered version of it, generally appears in the three lower voices. For example, the second "Kyrie eleison" has the *cantus firmus* material in the Tenor I and in the Bassus; the "Et incarnatus est" has this material in the Tenor II and the Bassus. Indeed, Regnart selected the Bassus part for most of the *Leise*-phrase reiterations in this Mass. The Cantus part does not often carry the *cantus firmus* material, since this voice is usually melodically contrasted with one of the lower voices. However, an exception to this general treatment does occur in the Sanctus, where the first phrase of the *cantus firmus* is presented in long note values by the uppermost voices. Regnart makes this presentation more dramatic by anticipating the *cantus firmus* melody in the Altus, Tenor II, Tenor I, and Bassus parts, in that order.

That Regnart was influenced by Castiglione's ideal of *sprezzatura* (the art of making the difficult seem effortless) can be seen in the elaboration of the *cantus firmus* material occuring in all five voices of this Mass. However, after the Altus part has presented its melodic anticipations of the *cantus firmus* material at the beginning of each section of the Mass, it generally functions as a filler voice. Complexity and variety are evidenced in the alternation between the presentation of all phrases of the *Leise* in their original order in one voice only (e.g., in the "Patrem, factorem coeli et terra" of the Credo and in the Sanctus), on the one hand, and the various migrant *cantus firmus* techniques on the other. Regnart's migrant *cantus firmus* techniques include: (1) the complete or almost complete presentation of the *Leise* phrases "in order" by various voices; (2) the complete or almost complete presentation of the *Leise* phrases, but not in their original order, by various voices; and (3) free treatment of the melodic material presented by the *cantus firmus*.

Imitative and harmonic techniques in Regnart's Missa IV

Strict imitative technique is scarce; it is applied with persistence only in the Benedictus. The "Et iterum venturus est" section of the Credo and the Agnus Dei have strict imitations only at their beginnings. However, a free pseudo-imitative technique is usually present throughout this Mass.

Regnart occasionally punctuates the linear complexity of the pseudo-imitative practice by introducing such homophonic features as the harmonic *Villanellen* sequences that occur in the *trium* of the Credo, "Et iterum venturus est," and that form distinct *caesurae* within the setting. Such use of *Villanellen* techniques reflects the compositional style of Regnart's time, and it is a feature of some of his other works also. The *Villanellen* technique involves use of three-voice sections (*tricinia*) that are characterized by series of sixth-chords followed by chords in root position. In Regnart's *Missa IV*, the *Villanellen* technique is used not as a satire, but as a serious interruption of the text (see, for example, the setting of "Et iterum venturus est"). Other homophonic writing also occurs at the beginning of certain sections of the Mass (e.g., the second Kyrie eleison), where it provides a contrast with the polyphonic sections.

Generally, there is no regular time pattern established for voice entrances. Similarities in the time intervals separating entrances of the various voices are more prevalent in the first part of the composition than in the last. When the first *Leise* phrase is heard in the "Christe eleison," three of the five voices enter within one measure of each other. Two of the five voices enter within one measure of each other in the first "Kyrie eleison," in the "Qui tollis peccata mundi," in "Patrem factorem," in the Sanctus, and in the Agnus Dei. There is no pattern established for voice entrances in the "Et incarnatus est," the "Crucifixus etiam," the "Et iterum venturus est," and the Benedictus.

Regnart's Mass on "Christ ist erstanden" is typical of Masses written in the second half of the sixteenth century. For example, the use of *noema reciprocae* figures, the insertion of a homophonic section in contrast to the polyphonic writing within the setting, and the use of Kyklosis figures must be seen as signs of Regnart's time. However, individualistic traits are manifested in the *Villanellen*-like homophony (this being a secular device); and even more unique to Regnart is the fact that the *cantus firmus* is often anticipated by a free counter-theme; when the *cantus firmus* is stated, it is often covered by a harmonic chordal texture that is of consequent importance for the whole setting.

Performance Practice

Suggestions of appropriate performance media are editorially supplied at the beginning of each polyphonic setting. Nos. 1, 2, and 3 should be performed by a small ensemble of six to eight performers, with instruments accompanying one or more vocal parts. In no. 5, the parts indicated by chorale notation could be performed by a vocal soloist or by the entire congregation. No. 17, likewise, could be performed by the entire congregation.

Certain aspects of performance in some of the settings in the present edition require further comment. In "Also heilig ist der Tag" (no. 1) the middle voice should be performed by tenor shawm or trombone. Since no text is given in its source, all four parts of "Dys synd die heylgen zehn gebot" (no. 2) could be performed by soprano, alto, tenor, and bass shawms, or by two oboes, English horn, and bassoon. The canonic relationship between the Altus I and Tenor of no. 4, "Christ ist erstanden" by Heugel, calls for a performance by the alto recorder and sackbutt or by a viola and trombone. Stressing the importance of the *cantus firmus*, the Tenor part of Raselius's "Gelobet seistu Jesu Christ" (no. 8) should be doubled by a tenor recorder or trombone. In Rasch's "Nun bitten wir den heiligen Geist" (no. 9), the presence of a great deal of contrapuntal motion in the four upper voices against a static *cantus firmus* suggests a performance by four recorders and portative organ, or by a woodwind quartet and violoncello.

Sources

With one exception, all the *Leise* settings of this edition were originally written in white notation. In its source manuscript the "Also heilig ist der Tag" setting (no. 1) is a luxurious example of black notation in which two tied semibreves of *Hufnagel*-like (horseshoe-shaped) figures indicate a brevis, two dots above a note require a repetition of that note, and a dot following a note means that the note is doubled in value.

As the following chart shows, manuscript sources far outnumber printed sources for the *Leise* settings. The reason for this may be that some set-

HANDWRITTEN AND PRINTED SOURCES FOR THE LEISE SETTINGS IN THIS EDITION[77]

COMPOSER	LEISE SETTING	SOURCE LOCATION	FORMAT
	Manuscripts		
Anonymous	Also heilig ist der Tag (1)	Zwickau, Vollhardt No. 15, 842, p. 156	Choir book
Anonymous	Dys synd die heylgen zehn gebot (2)	Munich, Cod. lat. 6034	Part books
Max Greiter	Christ ist erstanden/ Christus surrexit (3)	Basel, FXL. No. 102	Part books
Joan Heugel	Christ ist erstanden (4)	Kassel, Mus. 38, 43, 91	Part books
Anonymous	Christ ist erstanden/ Es giengen drey frauen (5)	Vienna, Mus. 16202, 16207, 16694, 19428	Choir book
Sigmund Hemmel	Gott sey gelobet vnd gebenedeiet (7)	Stuttgart, Cod. Mus. I, 6	Choir book
Balduin Hoyoul	Gott sey gelobet vnd gebenedeiet (10)	Stuttgart, Cod. I, 48	Choir book
Ludwig Daser	Christ lag in Todesbanden (11)	Stuttgart, Cod. Mus. I, 12	Choir book
Anonymous	Christus surrexit (12)	Munich, Ms. 31, No. 12	Choir book
Anonymous	Christ ist erstanden (13)	Munich, Ms. 31, No. 13	Choir book
Anonymous	Jesus Christus vero est agnus–Jesus Christus Vnser Heiland/ Gratia sit Deo– Christ ist erstanden (14)	Zwickau, Vollhardt No. 11	Part books
Anonymous	Nun bitten wir den heiligen Geist (15)	Zwickau, Vollhardt No. 273	Part books
Huldrich Braetel	In Gottes namen faren wir (17)	Munich, Pr. 156/18 19 May 1542	See Preface for description of format
	Prints		
Bartholomaeus Gesius	Mitten wir im leben sind (6)	British Museum	Modern score
Andreas Raselius	Gelobet seistu Jesu Christ (8)	Goettingen, Lib. Mus. Theol. 226	Modern score
Johannes Rasch	Nun bitten wir den heiligen Geist (9)	Augsburg, Stadtbibliotek	Part books
Christoph Thomas Walliser	Christ lag in Todesbanden (16)	Zwickau, Vollhardt, No. 134	Part books
Jacob Regnart	Missa IV: Christ ist erstanden (18)	Augsburg, Stadtbibliotek	Part books

tings were written for specific performances at court chapels (those by Hemmel, Heugel, and Hoyoul), and others, such as the "Jesus Christus vero est agnus-Jesus Christus Vnser Heiland/Gratia sit Deo-Christ ist erstanden" setting (no. 14) were conceived for specific local liturgies. All handwritten sources are unica except for "Christ ist erstanden/Es giengen drey frauen" (no. 5), of which there are four identical musical copies in the Österreichische Nationalbibliothek Vienna (see Critical Notes).

Although all of the sources, both printed and in manuscript, give fairly straightforward renderings of the *Leise* settings, two sources present this material in unusual forms. First, all parts of no. 15, "Nun bitten wir den heiligen Geist" (Zwickau, Vollhardt, No. 273), are accompanied by the complete text of two stanzas in the source print. However, the very first text line of the first stanza is missing in the source. Thus, all parts begin with "-lige Geist" or "Geist," with the exception of the two contralto parts, which begin with the complete statement of the second stanza "Du suesse lieb schenck vns deine huld." Second, the source manuscript of no. 17, the eight-part canon "In Gottes namen faren wir" (Munich Pr. 156/18), presents this music on a staff of six lines that is drawn in the shape of a circle. The first line of the text is indicated underneath the beginning of this composition, which is marked in the source by the tenor clef and the C signature, and all entrances of the different voices are indicated by means of an ·S· sign. The notes that occur on the sixth line of the staff used in this source normally would have been written on additional lines above the usual five-line staff. The manuscript gives no measure indications, and only the last longa (g) is framed by two barlines, which possibly may refer to its being sustained within the staff of six lines.

The Edition

Selection of Settings

The selection of settings for this publication has been based on a number of considerations. First, an attempt has been made to present at least one polyphonic setting of every *Leise* listed in the general repertory (see p. vii). However, settings of "Mensch willst du leben seliglich," "O du armer Judas," and "Sei willkommen" are not included in this edition, because modern transcriptions of their settings are already available.[78] Due to its importance, more than one setting of the "Christ ist erstanden" *Leise* has been included.

Second, settings have been chosen that are suitable for certain seasons of the church year (e.g., Christmas, Lent, Easter, and Pentecost). Some settings are related to such goals of the religious life as committment to God and living according to the ethics of the Ten Commandments and other sacred writings. An attempt has been made to select settings that will meet the needs of twentieth-century church musicians.

Third, because acquaintance with sixteenth-century polyphonic chorale settings has generally been limited, settings have been selected to familiarize performers with music by composers other than those represented in the well-known Rhaw collections.[79] The *Kantional*-styled settings have not been included here because they are simplistic, note-against-note settings.

Transcription

In this edition the note values of the source manuscripts, even for the black notation of "Also heilig ist der Tag," have been reduced by one-half. The original clefs, signatures, and position and duration of the first note are given in an incipit appearing at the beginning of each setting. Accidental-usage has been modernized. Ligatures are indicated by horizontal brackets. Text treatment in both underlay and titles reflects the spelling used in the sources. Punctuation and capitalization have been modernized.

Critical Notes

[1] *Also heilig ist der Tag* (Anonymous)

M. 21, Cantus, note 1 is a quarter. Mm. 32-34 (note 1) Cantus part is as follows:

[2] *Dys synd die heylgen zehn gebot* (Anonymous)

Mm. 48-49, Altus, text is "Kyrie leis," unlike other parts, which have "Kyrie eleison."

[4] *Christ ist erstanden* (Joan Heugel)

M. 11, Altus II, note 2 is c' (half-note). M. 40, Altus I, note 2 is g (quarter-note).

[5] *Christ ist erstanden/*
Es giengen drey frauen (Anonymous)

In the first stanza, codices 16202, 16207, 19428 have the word "aller"; 16694 has "alle." The word "wir" in codex 16202 is present as "bir" in the codices 16207, 16694, 19428. The "Kyrie eleison" formula is written in codex 16207 as "Kyrie eleison," in 16202 as "Kyrie leison," in 16694 as "Kyrie eleison," and in 19428 as "Kyrie leison." In the second stanza the words "wer," "wir," and "welt" appear in 16202, and the words "ber," "bir," and "bolt" appear in codices 16207, 16694, and 19428. The same substitution for w by b occurs in the next two stanzas in the same codices.

[6] *Mitten wir im leben sind* (Bartholomaeus Gesius)
M. 26, Tenor, note 1 is g. M. 33, Cantus, notes 1 and 2 are f' and e'.

[7] *Gott sey gelobet vnd gebenedeiet* (Sigmund Hemmel)
Mm. 17-18, Cantus, text is "Herre," unlike other parts, which have "Herr."

[14] *Jesus Christus vero est agnus–*
Jesus Christus Vnser Heiland/
Gratia sit Deo–Christ ist erstanden (Anonymous)
M. 12, Cantus I, final note is a'. Mm. 15-18 and 23-30, all parts, text is "abvit," instead of the more correct "absolvit." Mm. 120-124 (note 2), Altus part is as follows:

[17] *In Gottes namen faren wir* (Huldrich Braetel)
M. 26, Tenor IV, text is simply "Kyrie"; Tenors V-VIII, text completely lacks the usual "Kyrie eleison, Christe eleison" formula.

[18] *Missa IV: Christ ist erstanden* (Jacob Regnart)
Gloria—M. 43, Tenor II, note 2 is e'. M. 62, Altus, note 5 is g'. *Credo*—Mm. 27-28, Bassus part is as follows:

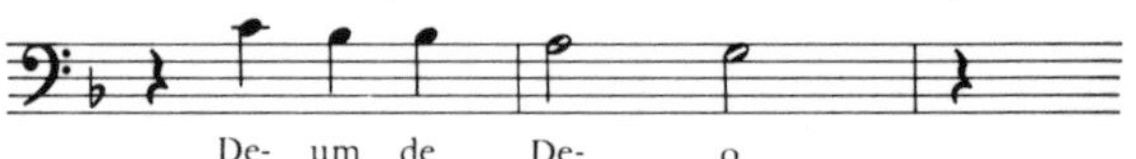

M. 42, Bass, final note (a) is tied to note 1 (a) of m. 43. M. 44, Altus, final note is divided into 2 eighths, both of which are b'-naturals. M. 47, Cantus, final note is g', tied to note 1 (g') of m. 48. M. 168, Bassus, note 2 is a. M. 152, Tenor II, note 3 is c'. M. 187, Tenor II, final note is e''. *Sanctus*—M. 14, Tenor II, note 3 is a.

Acknowledgments

I am grateful to Jane E. Rasmussen for her help in the preparation of this edition.

Johannes Riedel
May 1980 University of Minnesota

Notes

1. Johannes Riedel, "The History of the Monodic Leisen" (Research project, University of Southern California, Los Angeles, 1951).
2. Hans Joachim Moser, *Geschichte der deutschen Musik*, 2 vols. 4th ed. (Stuttgart: Cotta, 1921-1923), 1:150.
3. Heinrich August Hoffmann von Fallersleben, *Geschichte des deutschen Kirchenliedes bis auf Luthers Zeit*, 2nd ed. (Leipzig, 1848), p. 16. For the singing of "Kyrie eleison" cries after the ninth century, see Johannes Janota, *Studien zu Funktion und Typus des deutschen geistlichen Liedes im Mittelalter* (Munich: C. H. Beck, 1968), p. 151.
4. Franz Magnus Böhme, *Deutscher Liederhort* (Leipzig: Breitkopf & Härtel, 1893-1894), 3:671.
5. See the endings of nos. 3, 11, and 16 of this edition.
6. This is a favorite refrain in many sacred "Rufe" (cries) of the sixteenth and seventeenth centuries. Often, two refrains are used. After the second verse line there is a "Kyrie eleison," and after the fourth verse line there is an "Alleluia, gelobet..." refrain.
7. For the "Herr Gott erbarme dich unser" endings, and for many other "Kyrie eleison" variants, see Philipp Wackernagel, *Das deutsche Kirchenlied von der aeltesten Zeit bis zum Anfang des 17. Jahrhunderts*, vols. I-V (Leipzig, 1877). Some of these other endings are: Kyrie eleison; Kyrie eleyson; Kirioleyson, Kirieleison; Kirie eleyson; Kyrioleis, Kyryeleyson; Kyrieleison; Cirieleyson; Kyrie leyson; Kyrie leison, Kyrieleys; Kyrieleiss; Kyrie eleiss, Kirioleis; Kyrie; Kyrieleyson; Christeleyson, Kyrieleyson; Kyrie eleyson, Christe eleyson; Kyrie leison, Christe leyson; Kyrie Eleison, Christe Eleyson; Kyrieleyson, Christeleyson, Kyrieleyson, Christeleyson; Allelvia, Kirieleyson; Allelvja or Kyrie eleison, Gott genade vns; Hilff vnns aus aller Not; Gelobt sei Gott; Gott mit vnns.

8. Some of the other *Leisen* are discussed in Markus Jenny, "Kyrieleis und Hosianna," *Jahrbuch für Liturgik und Hymnologie* (Kassel: Johannes Stauda, 1969), 14:117.

9. This listing of the *Leise* texts and tunes is arranged alphabetically. Numbers in parentheses following certain *Leise* titles here and throughout the Preface indicate the position of settings of the *Leisen* in the present edition.

10. Each *Leise* tune has many variants. A typical example of the corresponding tunes was chosen from among these variants for presentation here.

11. Wilhelm Bäumker, *Das katholische deutsche Kirchenlied in seinen Singweisen* (1886; reprint ed., Hildesheim: Georg Olms, 1962), 1:524.

12. Hans Teuscher, *Christ ist erstanden* (Kassel: Bärenreiter, 1930), p. 5.

13. Johannes Zahn, *Die Melodien der deutschen evangelischen Kirchenlieder* (Gütersloh: Bertelsmann, 1888), 1:524.

14. Zahn, *Die Melodien*, 1:522/523.

15. Zahn, *Die Melodien*, 4:665.

16. Bäumker, *Das katholische deutsche Kirchenlied*, 1:572.

17. Walter Blankenburg, "Jesus Christus, unser Heiland, der den Tod überwand," *Jahrbuch für Liturgik und Hymnologie* (Kassel: Johannes Stauda, 1971), 16:151.

18. Zahn, *Die Melodien*, 1:526.

19. Walther Lipphardt, "Mitten wir im Leben sind," *Jahrbuch für Liturgik und Hymnologie* (Kassel: Johannes Stauda, 1963), 8:99.

20. Zahn, *Die Melodien*, 1:546.

21. Zahn, *Die Melodien*, 5:40.

22. Walther Lipphardt, "Das älteste deutsche Weihnachtslied," *Jahrbuch für Liturgik und Hymnologie* (Kassel: Johannes Stauda, 1959), 4:95. For additional information see Johannes Janota, *Studien zu Funktion*, pp. 280, 285.

23. This is a translation of the word "Lobgesang" as used in the preface to Johann Spangenberg, *Zwölff christliche Lobgesenge und Leissen* (Wittenberg: G. Rhaw, 1545).

24. For information on the ecclesiatical modes, read Donald J. Grout, *A History of Western Music* (New York: W. W. Norton, 1964), p. 26.

25. This melody is classified as Aeolian (Dorian) by Alfred Stier, "Zur musikalischen Gestalt des evangelischen Kirchenliedes" in Weismann, Ebergard and others, *Liederkunde Erster Teil: Lied 1 bis 175* (Göttingen: Vandenhoeck & Rupprecht, 1970), p. 43.

26. Alfred Stier, "Zur musikalischen Gestalt," p. 44.

27. For explanation of details of the bar form, consult Johannes Riedel, *The Lutheran Chorale: Its Basic Traditions* (Minneapolis: Augsburg Publishing, 1967), p. 41.

28. Walter Blankenburg, *Geschichte der Melodien des Evangelischen Kirchengesangbuchs* (Göttingen: Vandenhoeck & Rupprecht, 1957), p. 62.

29. Blankenburg, *Geschichte*, p. 62.

30. In addition to the five *Leisen* associated with the "Christ ist erstanden" *Leise*, one should mention three others whose melodies are marginally related to that of "Christ ist erstanden": "Es gingen drey frauen"; "Am Sabbath früh"; and "Es flog ein Täublein weisse." For the first, see no. 5 of this edition. For the latter two, see Walther Lipphardt, "Die älteste Ausgabe von Beuttners Gesangbuch, Graz 1605," *Jahrbuch für Liturgik und Hymnologie* (Kassel: Johannes Stauda, 1962), 7:143.

31. Heribert Ringmann and Joseph Klapper, *Das Glogauer Liederbuch. Erster Teil: Deutsche Lieder und Spielstücke*, Das Erbe Deutscher Musik, Vol. 4 (Kassel: Bärenreiter, 1936; reprint ed., 1954):4.

32. Johannes Rasch, *Cantivncvlae Paschales* (Munich: Adam Berg, 1572).

33. Zahn, *Die Melodien*, 4:257.

34. Konrad Ameln, Christhard Mahrenholz, and Wilhelm Thomas, *Handbuch der deutschen evangelischen Kirchenmusik* (Göttingen: Vandenhoeck & Rupprecht, 1950), 3:183. A similar melody is also given in Zahn, *Die Melodien*, 1:467. The "Surrexit Christus hodie" text is sometimes replaced by the "Surrexit Christus Dominus" text in the *Leise* literature.

35. Zahn, *Die Melodien*, 5:261/262.

36. Luther's "gebessert" version is included in *Geystliche Lieder* (Leipzig: Babst, 1545), no. 8.

37. See Johannes Riedel, "Leisen Formulae: Their polyphonic settings in the Renaissance and Reformation" (Ph.D. diss., University of Southern California, 1953), p. 362.

38. Johannes Janssen, *Geschichte des deutschen Volkes seit dem Ausgange des Mittelalters* (Freiburg, 1877), 1:290.

39. Ringmann and Klapper, *Das Glogauer Liederbuch*.

40. Georg Rhaw, *Newe Deudsche geistliche Gesenge*, ed. Johannes Wolf (Wittenberg, 1544; reprint ed. in DDT, 1908), 34:27.

41. Johannes Riedel, "Vocal Leisen settings in the Baroque Era," in *The Musical Heritage of the Lutheran Church*, ed. Theodore Hoelty-Nickel (St. Louis: Concordia Publishing House, 1959), 5:108.

42. Johannes Leisentritt, *Kurtzer Ausszug, Der Christlichen und Catholisch Gesaeng* (Dillingen, 1576).

43. Michael Praetorius, *Complete Works*, ed. Friedrich Blume, 19 vols. (Wolfenbüttel, Berlin: Kallmeyer, 1928-1949), 9: No. 30, p. 34.

44. Sankt Gallen, *Codex 430*, fol. 114r.

45. *Alte Catholische Geistliche Kirchengesaeng* (Koeln, 1600).

46. Johannes Plath, *Christ ist erstanden* (Leipzig, Hamburg: Gustav Fick, 1938).

47. Hoffmann von Fallersleben, *Geschichte des deutschen Kirchenliedes*, p. 354.

48. *Gesangbuch darinnen Psalmen vnnd geistliche Lieder* (Eisleben, 1598).

49. For further information concerning the coexistence of "Christ ist erstanden" and "Es giengen drey frauen," see Janota, *Studien zu Funktion*, pp. 181-182. Because "Es giengen drey frauen" is related to "Christ ist erstanden" only under certain circumstances, the "three Marys" *Leise* is not considered by the editor to be an "official" member of the "Christ ist erstanden" subgroup.

50. "Jesus Christus vero est agnus" and "Gratia sit Deo" are not *Leisen*. "Jesus Christus vero est agnus" is an *Agnus Dei* trope with an "Alleluia" ending. "Gratia sit Deo" is a liturgical formula that ends with an "Amen" statement. Neither is connected by text or tune with any of the twelve *Leisen* in the German repertoire. The use of "Jesus Christus vero est agnus" and "Gratia sit Deo" together with "Jesus Christus Vnser Heiland" and "Christ ist erstanden" is the result of a particular liturgical situation at a particular church.

51. An interesting account of the singing of the Christmas *Leise* "Sei willkommen Herre Christ" before the first Christmas Mass Proper is discussed in Janota, *Studien zu Funktion*, p. 112/113.

52. For the interpolation of the *Ascensionis Leise*, "Christ fuhr gen Himmel," within Notker Balbulus's sequence

"Summi triumphum Regis," see W. Crecelius, "Craislheimer Schulordnung von 1480 mit deutschen geistlichen Liedern," *Alemannia* (1875), p. 251.

53. For numerous uses of "Christ ist erstanden" and of "Mitten wir im leben sind" as sermon *Leisen*, see Janota, *Studien zu Funktion*, p. 74.

54. For an exceptional use of "Christ ist erstanden" at the occasion of the Elevation, read Janota, *Studien zu Funktion*, p. 169.

55. For an updated and elaborate discussion of the results of research on the use of "Christ ist erstanden" at the end of the *Visitatio sepulchri*, consult Janota, *Studien zu Funktion*, pp. 172-183.

56. Lipphardt, "Das älteste deutsche Weihnachtslied," p. 95.

57. Franz Magnus Böhme, *Deutscher Liederhort*, 3:627.

58. Arnold Schmitz, "Ein schlesisches Cantional aus dem 15. Jahrhundert," *Archiv für Musikforschung* I (1936):399.

59. For the many different uses of "Christ ist erstanden" see Walther Lipphardt, "Christ ist erstanden," *Jahrbuch für Liturgik und Hymnologie*, (Kassel: Johannes Stauda, 1961), 6:96.

60. Lipphardt, "Christ ist erstanden."

61. Ernst Schmidt, *Führer durch das Gesangbuch der Evangelisch-Lutherischen Kirche in Bayern rechts des Rheines* (Erlangen: Martin Luther Verlag, n. d.), p. 61.

62. Julius Smend, *Die evangelischen deutschen Messen bis zu Luthers deutscher Messe* (Göttingen: Vandenhoeck & Ruprecht, 1896), p. 9.

63. Luther's *Missa Formula* suggests it.

64. Hermann Peppen, *Das erste Kurpfälzer Gesangbuch und seine Singweisen* (M. Schauenberg), p. 7.

65. The didactic *Leisen* were also prescribed for seasons of the Church year. For example, a Lutheran church order from Annaberg, 1579, prescribes "Dys synd die heylgen zehn gebot" and "Mensch willst dů leben seliglich" for Sundays after Trinity; the first for the 18th, and the second for the 5th, 6th, 16th, 17th, and 22nd Sundays after Trinity.

66. See Lipphardt, "Christ ist erstanden," p. 96 and note 54.

67. Johannes Riedel, "Leisen Formulae," p. 500.

68. "Mitten wir im leben sind" is not listed here, since it is derived from an antiphon ("Media vita") rather than from a sequence.

69. For other combinations of sequence and *Leise*, see Johannes Riedel, "Christ ist erstanden," *The Hymn* 8, no. 1 (1957):17.

70. Heribert Ringmann, "Das Glogauer Liederbuch (um 1480)," *Zeitschrift für Musikwissenschaft* XV (November 1932):49.

71. Johannes Riedel, "Leisen Formulae," p. 500.

72. Friedrich Blume, ed., *Johannes Hehnel (Galliculus)*, Das Chorwerk, vol. 44 (Wolfenbüttel, Berlin: Kallmeyer, 1937):2.

73. See p. x for specific information concerning the *Leisen* associated with "Christ ist erstanden."

74. Blume, ed., *Johannes Hehnel (Galliculus)*, p. 2

75. Friedrich Blume, *Die evangelische Kirchenmusik* (Potsdam: Athenaion, 1932), p. 62.

76. Johann, Gottfried Walther, *Musikalisches Lexikon* (Leipzig, 1732), p. 516. The translation and correction of the Latin text was provided by William L. Smith:

> Eheu Destituor viribus, languescunt corporis membra, inopinata me corripit infirmitas, stratum lectuli mei quaorere cogor, mens mea ingentem praesagit mihi calmitatem futuram, aut morte cito solvar, aut diuturmum vitae poriculum sustinere impellor, nisi fallor, tempus resolutionis meae jam modo instabit, disacendum nihi esse video, haec ultima manus mea his ultimis operibus mais imponenda est, satis hactenus cecini, satis cantionum composui, satis mundo vixi.

77. A variety of styles existed concurrently during the sixteenth century. Often, more than one style occurs in the same composition. For instance, nos. 5, 6, 7, and 8, and nos. 10 and 11 show *Kantional* settings in combination with a *cantus firmus* presentation. Thus, an attempt has been made here to present the succession of settings according to such stylistic criteria rather than according to purely chronological criteria. Huldrich Braetel's "In Gottes namen faren wir" (17), written in 1542, could have been placed after Joan Heugel's "Christ ist erstanden" (4), which was written in 1541. However, Braetel's simple canon fits better at the end than at the beginning for stylistic reasons. Moreover, the order of Balduin Hoyoul's "Gott sey gelobet vnd gebenedeiet" and Ludwig Daser's "Christ lag in Todesbanden" could have been reversed, since both show an interesting mingling of *Kantional* and *cantus firmus* writing. Numbers in parentheses indicate the position of a given setting within the edition.

78. For a listing and discussion of these settings as they are available in modern editions, see Johannes Riedel "Leisen Formulae," pp. 692-704.

79. Georg Rhaw, *Neue deutsche Geistliche (1544)*, ed. Johannes Wolf (Denkmäler Deutsche Tonkunst: Breitkopf & Härtel, 1908), vol. 34.

Texts and Translations

In the texts of the *Leise* settings given below, the repetition of verse lines in various parts of the score is not given. The translations, which are by the editor, are presented only in order to acquaint the reader with the spirit of the original texts. Because it is the standard Mass text, the underlay of Regnart's *Missa IV* is not presented in this section.

[1] Also heilig ist der Tag
Anonymous

Also heilig ist der Tag
Das ihn niemand mit Lob erfüllen mag
Alleluia Alleluia Alleluia
Und der einzige Gottessohn
Der die Hölle zerbrach
Und den leidigen Teufel darinnen fand
Alleluia, Alleluia, Alleluia, Alleluia.

(Thus the day is holy
nobody can praise it enough
Alleluia, Alleluia, Alleluia
Only God's son
broke hell to pieces
with the very devil in it.
Alleluia, Alleluia, Alleluia, Alleluia.)

[2] Dys synd die heylgen zehn gebot
Anonymous

Dys synd die heylgen zehn gebot,
die vnns gab vnser herre Gott,
durch Mosen seinen diener trew,
hoch auff dem berg Sinay,
Kyrie eleison, Kyrie eleison.

(These are the holy ten commands,
which our Lord God gave us
through Moses, his loyal servant,
high up on Mount Sinai,
Kyrie eleison, Kyrie eleison.)

[3] Christ ist erstanden/Christus surrexit
Max Greiter (1490-1550)

Christ ist erstanden,
von der marter alle,
dess sollen wir alle fro sein,
Christ sol vnser trost sein.
Alleluia, Alleluia.

Christus surrexit,
mala nostra texit,
et quos hoc dilexit,
nos ad coelos vexit.
Alleluia, Alleluia, Alleluia, Alleluia.

(Christ is arisen
from all the tortures,
wherefore let us joyful be,
Christ be our consolation.
Alleluia, Alleluia.

Christ is arisen
he paid with his life for our sins,
he lifted us toward heaven
for which we love him most.
Alleluia, Alleluia, Alleluia, Alleluia.)

[4] Christ ist erstanden
Joan Heugel (before 1500-1585)

Christ ist erstanden,
Von der marter alle.
Des sol wir alle fro sein.
Christ sol unser trost sein.
Kyrie eleison.

(Christ is arisen
from all the tortures,
wherefore let us joyful be.
Christ be our consolation.
Kyrie eleison.)

[5] Christ ist erstanden/Es giengen drey frauen
Anonymous

Christ ist erstanden
Von der marter aller.
Des sollen bir alle fro sein.
Christ sol vnser trost sein.
Kyrie eleison.

Vnd ber er nit erstanden,
Die belt die ber zergangen,
Vnd seit das er erstanden ist,

So loben bir den herren Jesu Christ.
Kyrie eleison.

Es giengen drey frauen,
Sie bolten das grab beschauen.
Da ruefft der Engel helle:
"Bas suchet jhr frauen so schöne?

So ist er ye erstanden,
Den jhr da boltet salben."
Kyrie eleison.

Alleluia, Alleluia,
Das sollen bir alle fro sein,
Christ sol vnser trost sein.
Kyrie eleison.

(Christ is arisen
from all the tortures.
Wherefore let us joyful be.
Christ be our consolation.
Kyrie eleison, Kyrie eleison.

Had he not arisen,
the world would have ended,
but he has arisen,
so we praise the Lord Jesus Christ.
Kyrie eleison.

There went three women,
they wanted to see the tomb.
There the angel cried with a loud voice:
"Whom do Thou seek, you lovely women?
He is already risen,
whom you wanted to see now."
Kyrie eleison.

Alleluia, Alleluia
So let us all rejoice,
Christ be our consolation,
Kyrie eleison.)

[6] Mitten wir im leben sind
Bartholomaeus Gesius (ca. 1555-1613)

Mitten wir im leben sind
Mit dem todt vmbfangen:
Wen suchen wir der hilffe thut
Das wir gnad erlangen?
Das bistu, Herr, alleine.
Vns rewet vnser missethat,
Die dich, Herr Gott, erzürnet hat.

Heiliger Herre Gott,
Heiliger starcker Gott,
Heiliger Barmherziger Heiland,
Du ewiger Gott!
Las vns nicht versenken
In des bittern todesnoth!
Kyrie eleison.

(Amidst life we are
surrounded by death:
Whom do we seek who provides aid
that we may obtain mercy?
It is Thou alone, Lord God,
We repent for our sins,
which so angered Thee, Lord God.

Holy Lord God,
Holy strong God,
Holy compassionate Saviour,
Thou eternal God!
Let us not be overcome
in the flood of bitter death!
Kyrie eleison.)

[7] Gott sey gelobet vnd gebenedeiet
Sigmund Hemmel (d. 1564)

Gott sey gelobet vnd gebenedeiet,
Der vns selber hat gespeiset
Mit seinem fleische vnd mit seinem bluete.
Das gib vns Herr Gott zu guete,
Kyrieleison.

Herr durch deinen heiligen leichnam,
Der von deiner muetter Maria kam,
Vnd das heilige bluet,
Hilff vns Herr aus aller nott.
Kyrieleison.

(God be praised and blessed,
who has himself nourished us
with his flesh and with his blood.
Thus gave to us Lord God our blessing,
Kyrieleison.

Lord through Thy sacred body,
from Thy mother Mary came,
and Thy sacred blood,
Save us Lord, from all distress.
Kyrieleison.)

[8] Gelobet seistu Jesu Christ
Andreas Raselius (1562-1602)

Gelobet seistu Jesu Christ,
Dass du mensch geboren bist,
Von einer Jungfrau das ist war,
Dess frewet sich der Engel schar.
Kyrie eleison.

(Praised be Thou Jesus Christ,
that you have chosen to become as man,
from a virgin this is true,
the multitude of angels rejoice.
Kyrie eleison.)

[9] Nun bitten wir den heiligen Geist
Johannes Rasch (1540-1612)

Nun bitten wir den heiligen Geist
Vmb den rechten glauben allermeist,
Dass er vns behüte an vnserm ende.
wenn wir heimfarn aus disem elende.
Kyrie eleison.

(Now we pray to the Holy Ghost
for the true faith,
that He protect us at our end,
when we go home from this vale of misery.
Kyrie eleison.)

[10] Gott sey gelobet vnd gebenedeiet
Balduin Hoyoul (1547-1652)

Gott sey gelobet vnd gebenedeiet,
Der vns selber hat gespeiset
Mit seinem fleische vnd mit seinem blüte.
Das gib vns Herr Gott zu güte,
Kyrie eleison.

Herr durch deinen heiligen leichnam,
Der von deiner Mütter Maria kam,
Vnd das heilige blüt,
Hilff vns herr auss aller not.
Kyrie eleison.

(God be praised and blessed,
who has himself nourished us
with his flesh and with his blood.
Thus gave to us Lord God our blessing
Kyrie eleison.

Lord through Thy sacred body,
from Thy mother Mary came,
and Thy sacred blood,
Save us Lord, from all distress.
Kyrie eleison.)

[11] Christ lag in Todesbanden
Ludwig Daser (1525-1589)

Christ lag in Todesbanden,
Für vnser sünd gegeben.
Der ist wieder erstanden
Vnd hat vns bracht das leben.
Das wir sollen frölich sein:
Gott loben vnd danckbar sein.
Vnd singen Alleluia!

(Christ lay in bonds of death,
given for our sins.
He is risen again
and brought us life.
Wherefore let us joyful be:
praise God and thankful be,
And sing Alleluia!)

[12] Christus surrexit
Anonymous

Christus surrexit,
mala nostra texit
et quos hic dilexit
nos ad coelos vexit.
Kirie eleison.

(Christ is arisen,
he paid with his life for our sins,
he lifted us toward heaven
for which we love him most.
Kirie eleison.)

[13] Christ ist erstanden
Anonymous

Christ ist erstanden
von der marter alle,
des sol wir alle fro sein,
Christ sol vnser trost sein.
Kyrie eleison.

(Christ is arisen
from all the tortures
wherefore let us joyful be,
Christ be our consolation.
Kyrie eleison.)

[14] Jesus Christus vero est agnus-Jesus Christus Vnser Heiland/Gratia sit Deo-Christ ist erstanden
Anonymous

Jesus Christus vero est agnus,
qui abvit peccata mundi,
qui mortem moriendo destruxit.
Kyrieleison,
et vitam resurgendo reparavit.
Alleluia.

Jesus Christus Vnser Heiland,
der den todt vberwandt,

ist aufferstanden.
Die sünd hat er gefangen.
Kyrie eleison.

[*Altera pars*]
Gratia sit Deo
qui dedit nobis victoriam
per Jesum Christum Dominum nostrum, Amen.

Christ ist erstanden
Von der Marter allen,
Des sollen wir alle froh sein,
Christ wil vnser trost sein.
Kyrieleis.

(Christ Jesus is the true Lamb,
who took away from us the sins of the world,
who destroyed death through his sacrifice at the cross,
Kyrie eleison,
and renewed our life through his resurrection.
Alleluia.

Jesus Christ our Savior,
who vanquished death,
is risen again.
He captured sin.
Kyrie eleison.

[*Altera pars*]
Thanks be to God
who gave us victory
through Christ Jesus our Lord, Amen.

Christ is arisen
from all the tortures
wherefore let us joyful be,
Christ be our consolation.
Kyrieleis.)

[15] Nun bitten wir den heiligen Geist
Anonymous

Nun bitten wir den heiligen Geist
Vmb den rechten glauben allermeist,
Das ehr vns behüte an vnserm Ende,
Wenn wir heimfaren aus diesem Elende.
Kyrie eleison.

(Now we pray to the Holy Ghost
for the true faith,
that He protect us at our end,
when we go home from this vale of misery.
Kyrie eleison.)

[16] Christ lag in Todesbanden
Christoph Thomas Walliser (1568-1648)

Christ lag in Todesbanden,
Für vnser Sund gegeben.
Der ist wieder erstanden
Vnd hat vns bracht das leben.
Das wir sollen fröhlich sein:
Gott loben vnd danckbar sein.
Vnd singen Alleluia!

(Christ lay in bonds of death,
given for our sins.
He is risen again
and brought us life.
Wherefore let us joyful be:
praise God and thankful be,
and sing Alleluia!)

[17] In Gottes namen faren wir
Huldrich Braetel (1495-1544)

In Gottes namen faren wir,
seiner genaden begeren wir,
Das helff vns die gotteskrafft
vnd das heylige grab, da Gott lag,
Kyrieleison, Christe eleison.

(We go forth in the name of God,
We need His mercy,
God's strength be of help to us
and the holy tomb, where God had lain,
Kyrie eleison, Christe eleison.)

LEISE SETTINGS
OF THE RENAISSANCE AND
REFORMATION ERA

[1] Also heilig ist der Tag

Anonymous

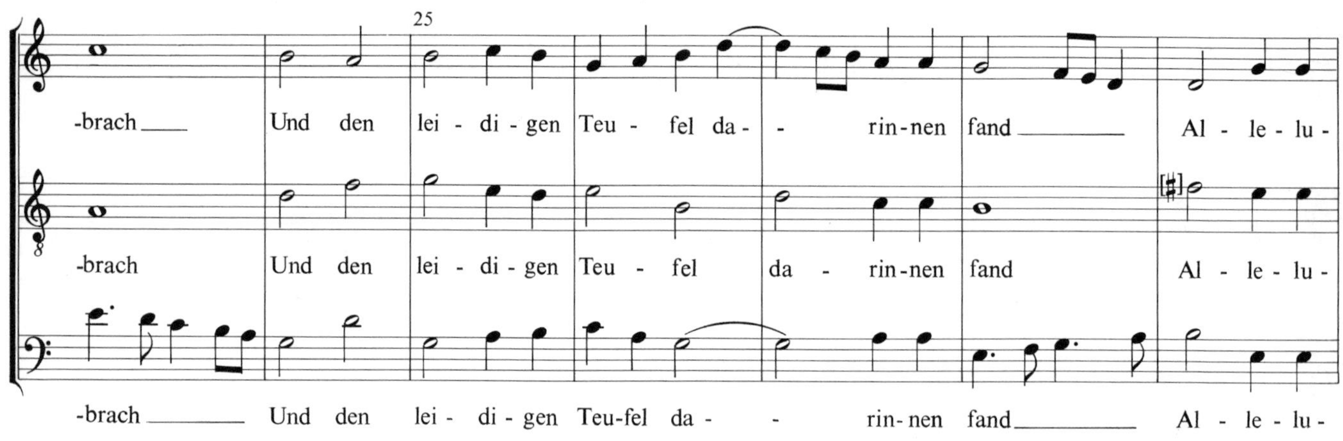

[2] Dys synd die heylgen zehn gebot

Anonymous

10
zehn ge - bot, die vnns gab vn-ser her - re Gott, vnns
- gen zehn ge - -bot, die vnns gab vn - ser her - re Gott, vnns gab vn - ser her -
synd die heyl - gen zehn ge - bot, die vnns gab vn - ser
- bot, die vnns gab vn- -ser her - - re Gott, die vnns gab vn - ser her-re Gott, vn -
15
gab vn - ser her - re Gott, durch Mo - -sen sei - - - nen die - ner
- re Gott, vnns gab vn -ser her - re Gott, durch Mo - sen sei - nen
her - re Gott, durch Mo - sen sei - nen die - ner
- ser her - re Gott, die vnns gab vn - ser Gott, durch Mo - sen sei -
20
trew, hoch auff dem berg Si - nay, hoch auff dem berg, hoch auff dem berg
die - -ner trew, hoch auff dem berg Si - -nay,
trew, hoch auff dem berg Si - -nay,
- nen die- - ner trew, hoch auff dem berg, auff dem berg Si - -nay, auff
[♭]

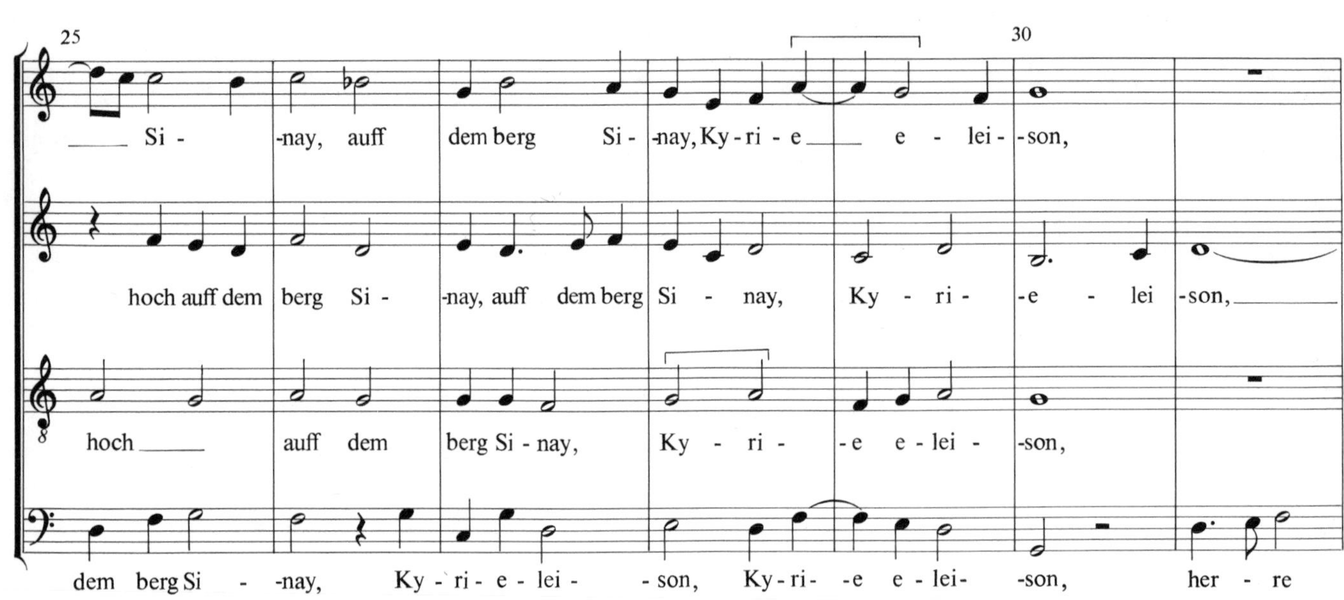
25
30
Si - -nay, auff dem berg Si - -nay, Ky - ri - e e - lei - -son,
hoch auff dem berg Si - -nay, auff dem berg Si - nay, Ky - ri - -e - lei -son,
hoch auff dem berg Si - nay, Ky - ri - -e e - lei - -son,
dem berg Si - -nay, Ky - ri - e - lei - - son, Ky - ri - -e e - lei - -son, her - re

35
her - re Gott, durch Mo - -sen sei - -
her - -re Gott, durch Mo - sen sei - nen
her - re Gott, her - re Gott, durch Mo - sen sei - nen
Gott, durch Mo- sen sei - - nen, sei - - nen die - ner trew, sei -

40
- nen die - ner trew, hoch auff dem berg Si - - -nay, hoch auff dem berg
die - - -ner trew, hoch auff dem,
die - ner trew, hoch auff dem berg Si - -nay,
- nen die - ner trew, hoch auff dem berg Si - -nay, auff

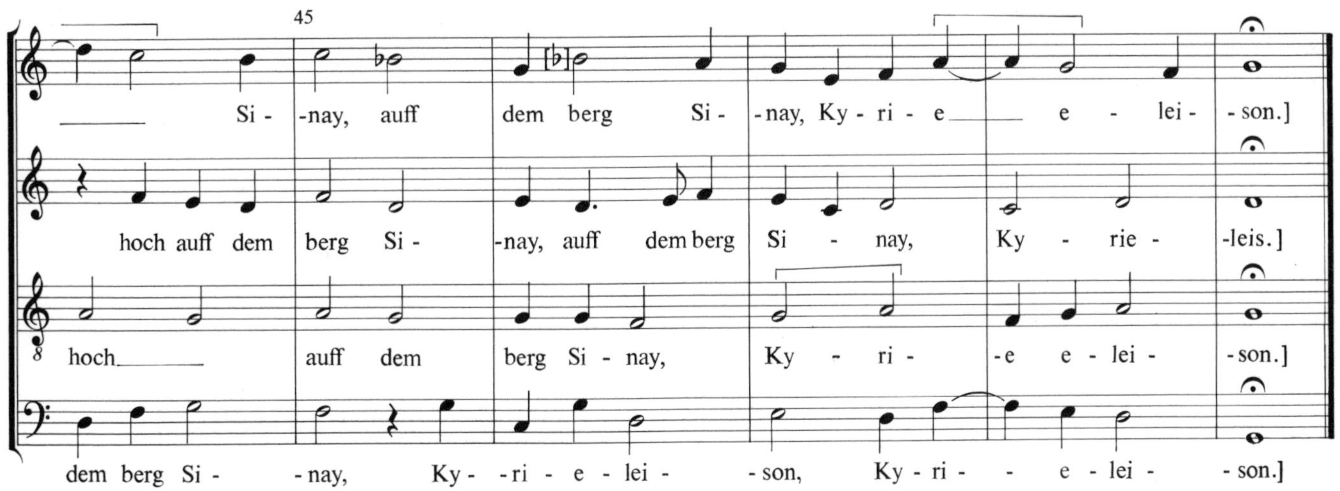

[3] Christ ist erstanden / Christus surrexit

Max Greiter
(1490–1550)

[CANTUS]
[ALTUS]
[VAGANS]
[BASSUS]

5
Christ ist er - - stan -
Chri - -stus sur - -re - - xit, ma - - la no - stra
Chri - - stus
Chri - - stus sur - re - - xit,

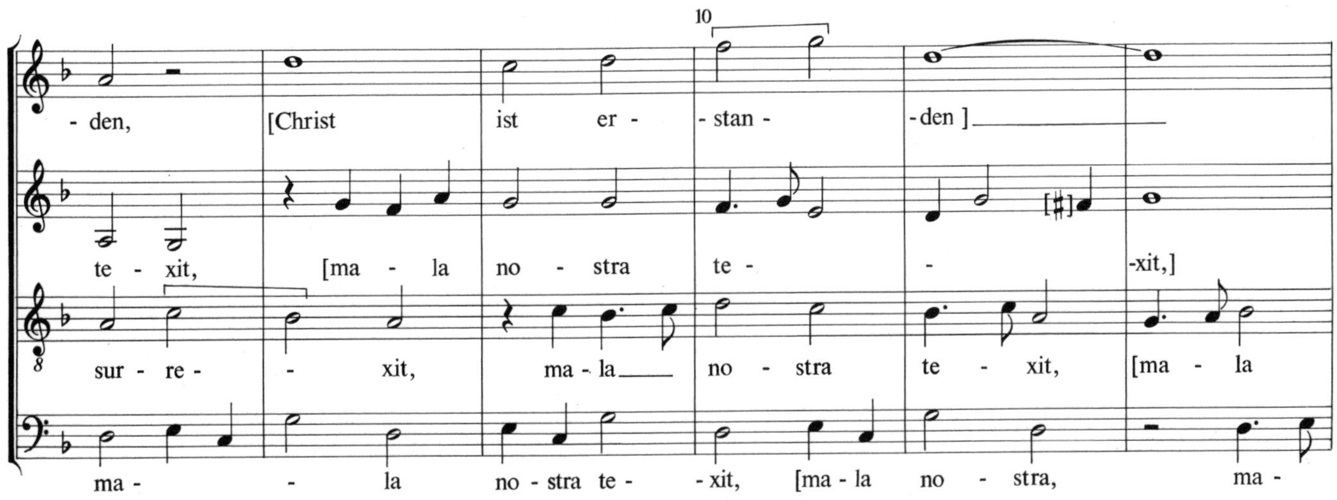

10
- den, [Christ ist er - - stan - - den]
te - xit, [ma - la no - stra te - - -xit,]
sur - re - - xit, ma - la no - stra te - xit, [ma - la
ma - - la no - stra te - - xit, [ma - la no - stra, ma -

15
von der mar- -ter al- -le,
ma- la no- stra te- xit, [ma- la no- stra te- -xit,]
no- stra, [ma- la no- stra te- -xit,] et
- la no- stra te- - - xit,]

20
dess sol- len wir al- -le
et quos hoc di- le- -xit, di- le-
quos hoc di- -le- xit, [di- - le- - -xit, di-
et quos hoc di- le- -xit, di- le- -

25
30
fro sein, Christ sol
- xit, di- -le- -xit nos ad coe-
-le- xit,] fro sein,
- xit, [nos ad coe- -los ve- xit,] nos ad coe- - los

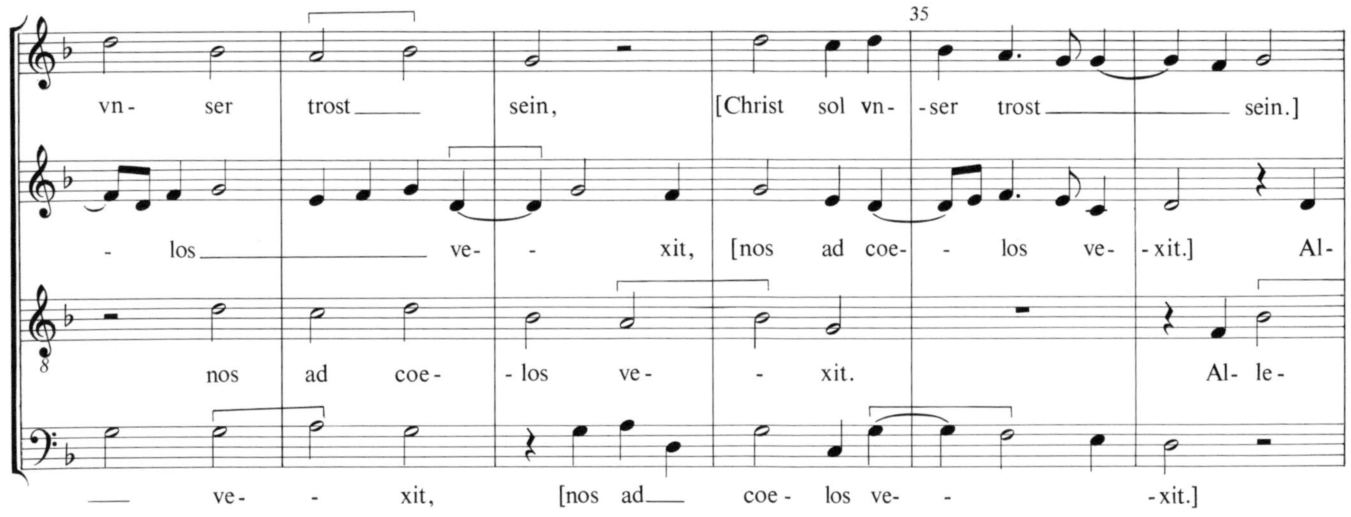
35
vn- ser trost sein, [Christ sol vn- -ser trost sein.]
- los ve- - xit, [nos ad coe- - los ve- -xit.] Al-
nos ad coe- -los ve- - xit. Al- le-
ve- - xit, [nos ad coe- los ve- - -xit.]

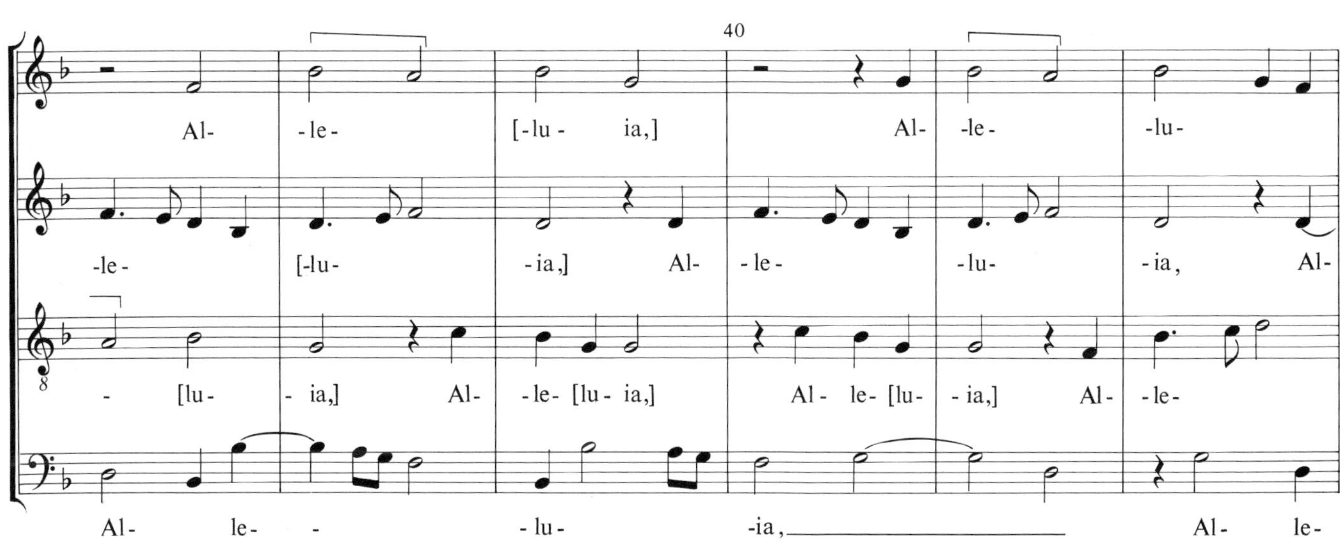
40
Al- -le- [-lu - ia,] Al- -le- -lu-
-le- [-lu- -ia,] Al- -le- -lu- -ia, Al-
- [lu- - ia,] Al- - le- [lu - ia,] Al - le- [lu- - ia,] Al- - le-
Al- le- - - lu- -ia, Al- le-

45
- - ia.
- le- lu- -ia, Al- -le- lu- - ia.
- - lu- - - ia.
[-lu- - ia,] Al- - le- lu- - - ia.

[4] Christ ist erstanden

Joan Heugel
(before 1500–1585)

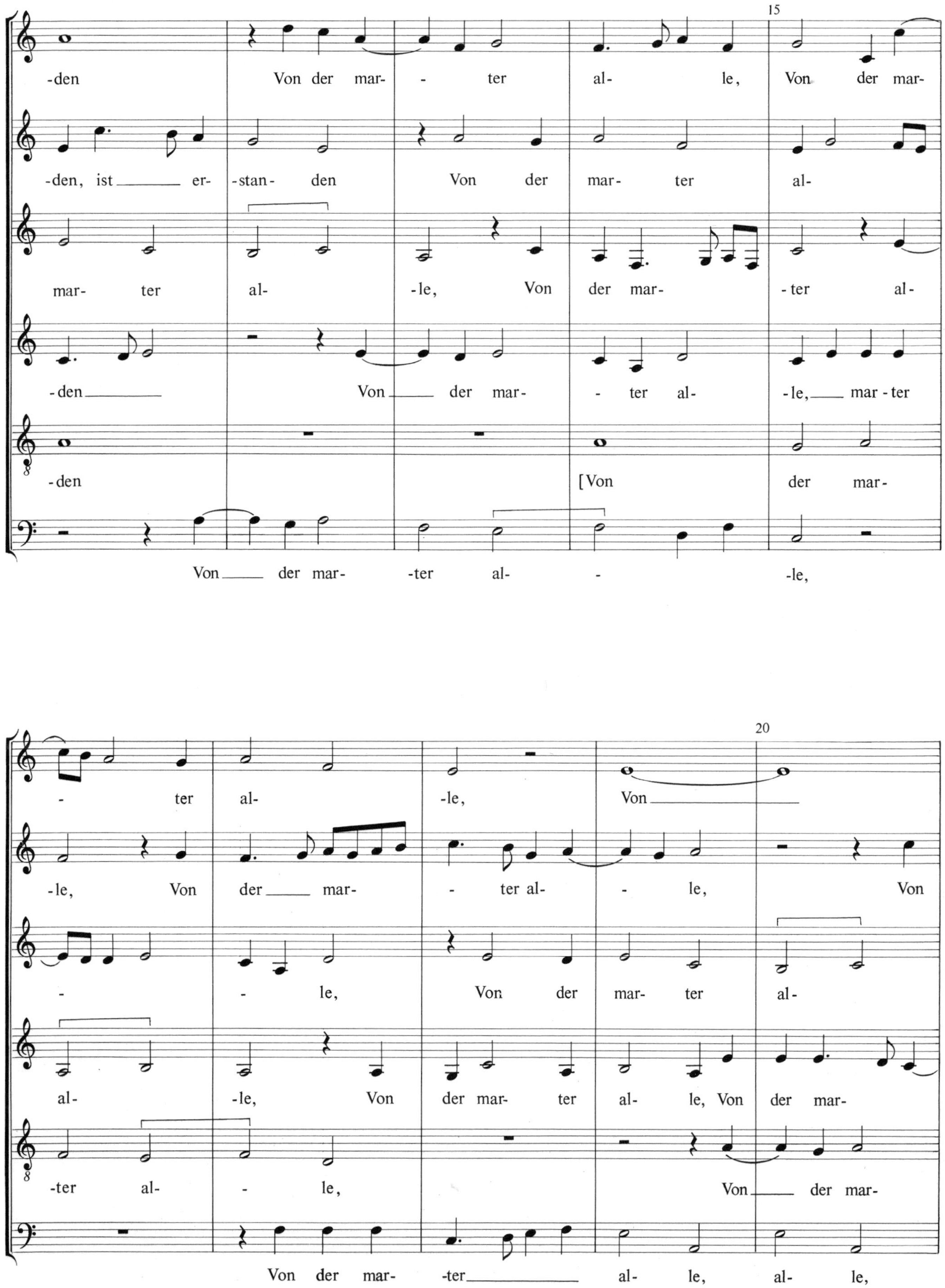

15

-den Von der mar- - ter al- le, Von der mar-
-den, ist er- -stan- den Von der mar- ter al-
mar- ter al- -le, Von der mar- -ter al-
-den Von der mar- - ter al- -le, mar-ter
-den [Von der mar-
Von der mar- -ter al- - -le,

25
der marter al- - le. Des sol wir al- le
der mar- - ter al- -le. Des sol wir al-
-le. Des sol wir al- -le fro sein,
- ter al- -le. Des sol wir al- le fro
-ter al- - le. Des sol wir al- - le
Von der mar- ter al- -le. Des sol wir,

30
fro sein. Des sol wir al- le, Des sol
- le fro sein. Des sol wir al- - le fro sein,
Des sol wir al-
sein, Des sol wir al- le, al- - le
fro sein,
Des sol wir al- - le fro sein,

35
wir al- - le, Des sol wir al- -le fro
Des sol wir al- -le fro sein. Christ sol
- le fro sein. Christ sol un- ser
fro sein, Des sol wir al- le fro sein.
Des sol wir al- -le fro sein. Christ
Des sol wir al - le fro sein, Des sol wir al- le

40
sein. Christ sol un- -ser trost
un- ser, Christ sol un- -ser trost sein, Christ
trost sein, Christ sol
Christ sol un- ser trost sein, Christ sol un- ser
sol un - -ser trost sein,
fro sein. Christ sol un- ser trost sein, Christ sol

45
sein, Christ sol un- -ser, Christ sol un- - ser trost
sol un- ser trost sein. Christ sol un- - ser
un- ser trost sein, Christ sol un- ser trost
trost sein, Christ sol un- ser trost
Christ sol un- ser trost sein.
un- ser trost sein, Christ sol un- -ser trost sein.

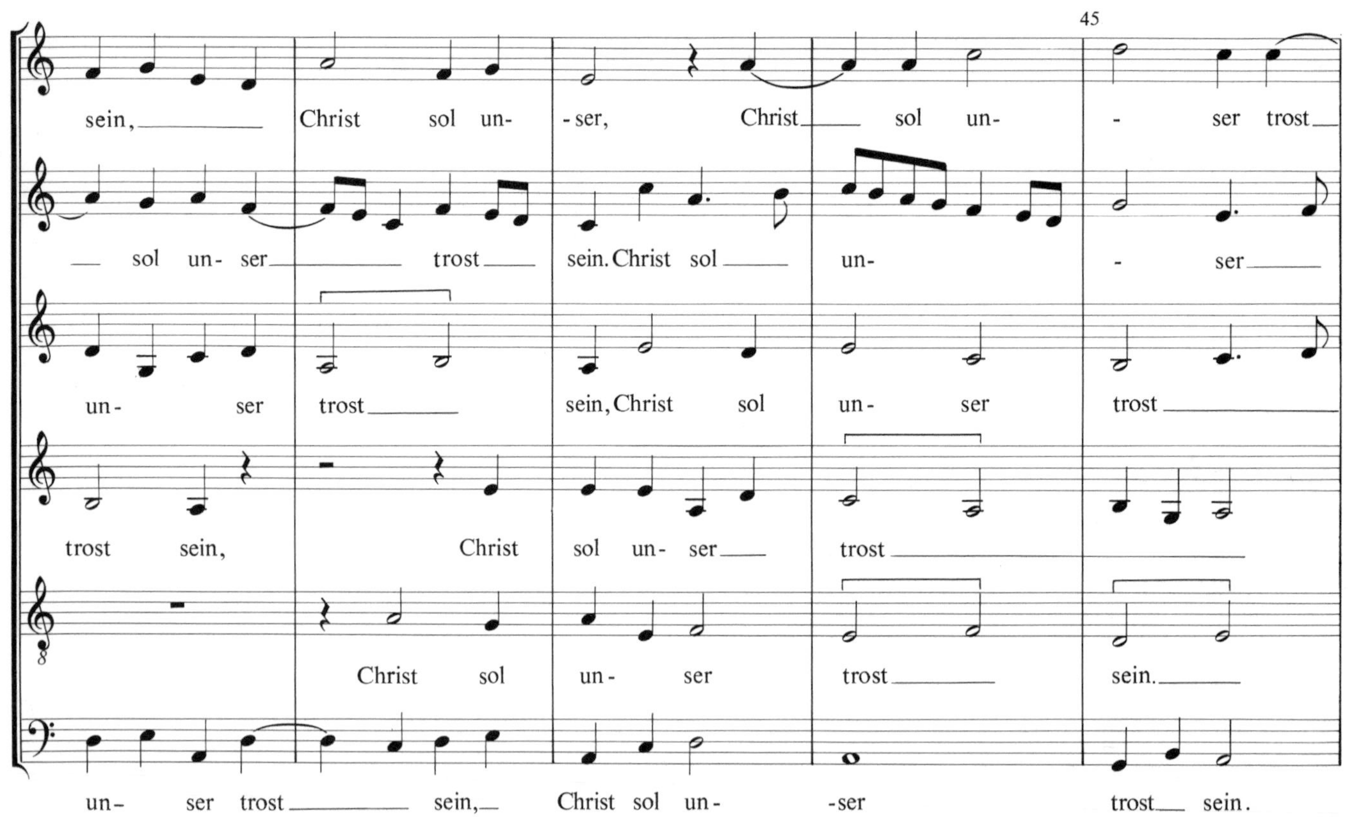

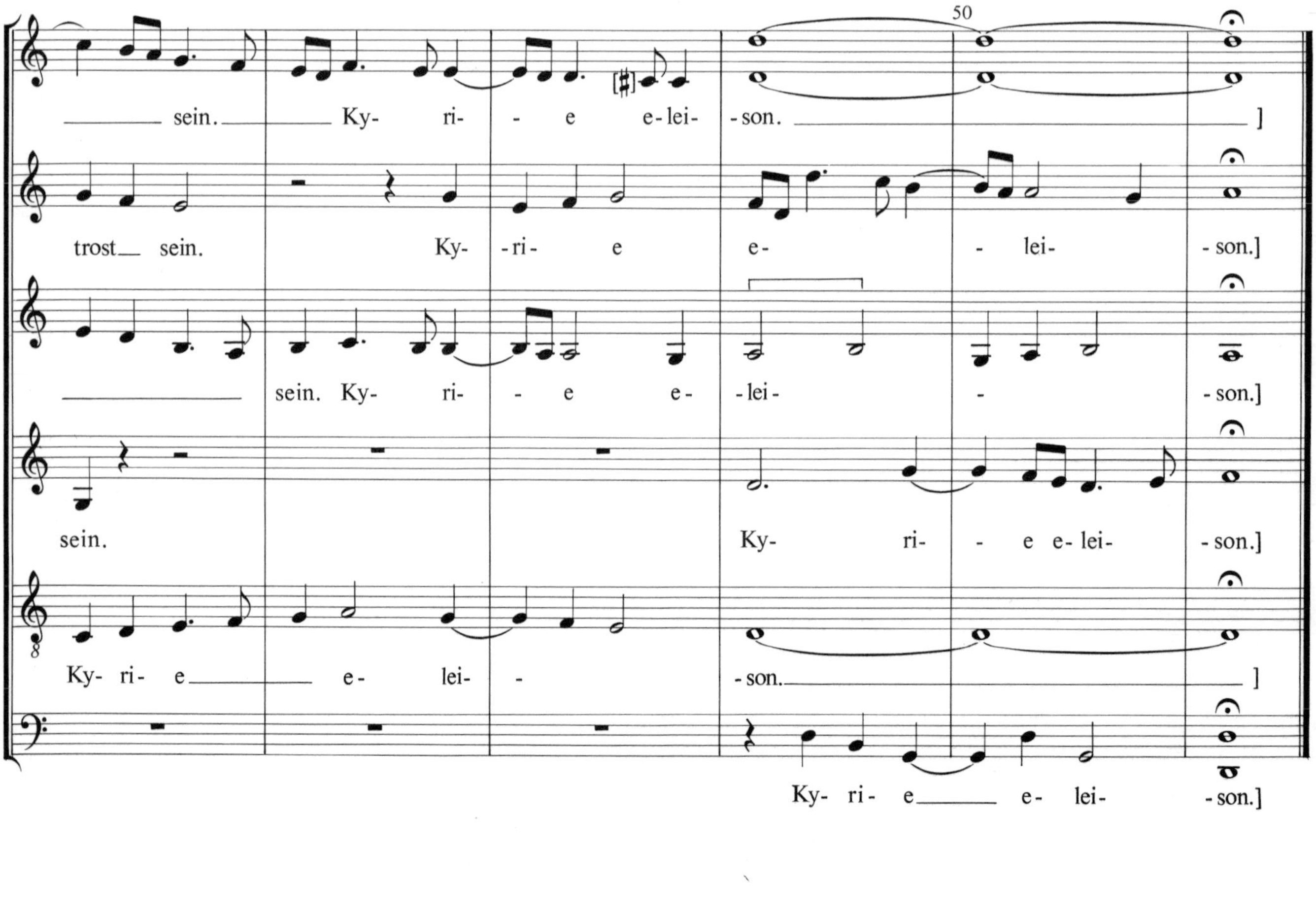

50
sein. Ky- ri- - e e- lei- - son.]
trost sein. Ky- - ri- e e- - lei- - son.]
sein. Ky- ri- - e e- - lei - - - son.]
sein. Ky- ri- - e e- lei- - son.]
Ky- ri- e e- lei- - - son.]
Ky- ri- e e- lei- - son.]

[5] Christ ist erstanden / Es giengen drey frauen

Anonymous

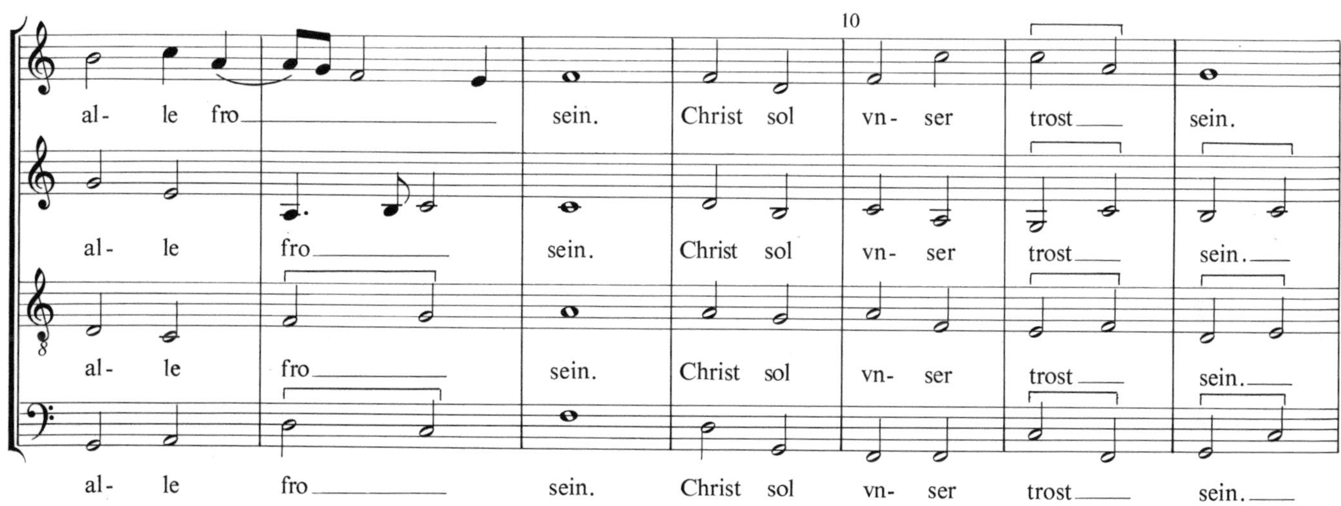

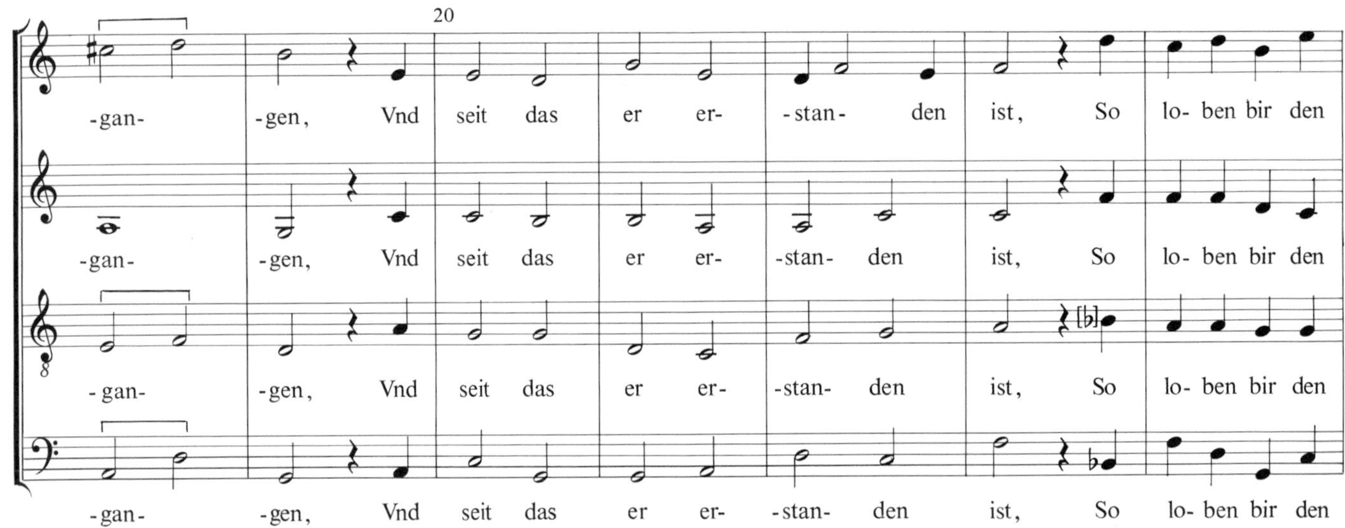
20
-gan- -gen, Vnd seit das er er- -stan- den ist, So lo- ben bir den
-gan- -gen, Vnd seit das er er- -stan- den ist, So lo- ben bir den
-gan- -gen, Vnd seit das er er- -stan- den ist, So lo- ben bir den
-gan- -gen, Vnd seit das er er- -stan- den ist, So lo- ben bir den

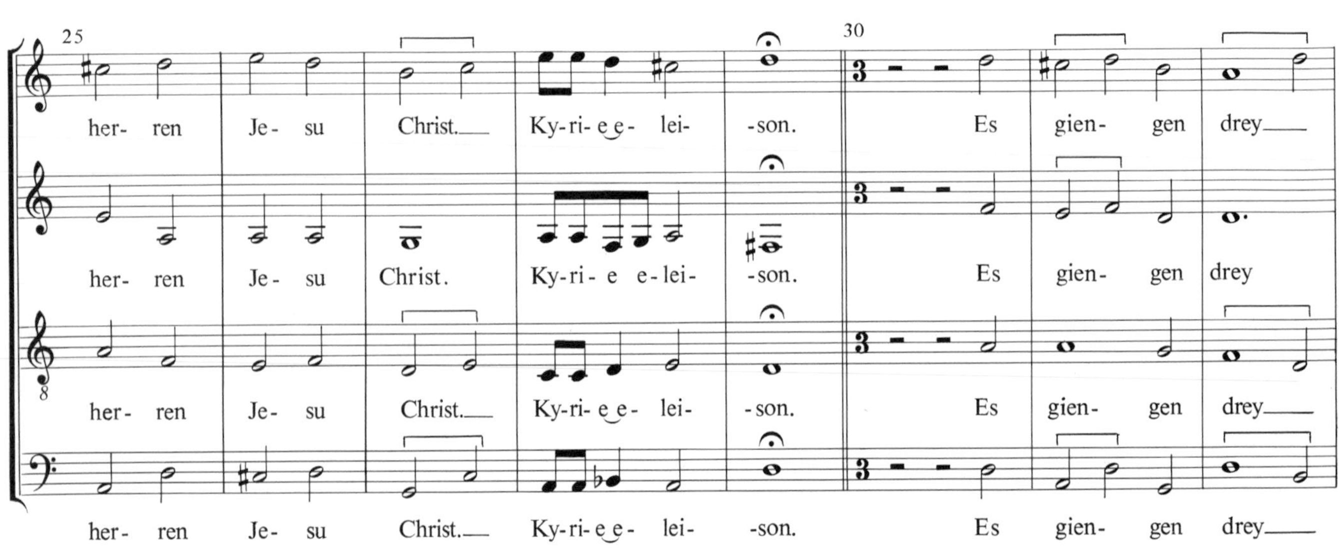
25
30
her- ren Je- su Christ. Ky-ri- e e- lei- -son. Es gien- gen drey
her- ren Je- su Christ. Ky-ri- e e- lei- -son. Es gien- gen drey
her- ren Je- su Christ. Ky-ri- e e- lei- -son. Es gien- gen drey
her- ren Je- su Christ. Ky-ri- e e- lei- -son. Es gien- gen drey

35
frau- -en, Sie bol- ten das grab be- -schau- -en. Da ruefft der
frau- -en, Sie bol- ten das grab be- -schau- -en. Da ruefft der
frau- -en, Sie bol- ten das grab be- -schau- -en. Da ruefft der
frau- -en, Sie bol- ten das grab be- -schau- -en. Da ruefft der

40
45
En- gel hel- -le: "Bas su- chet jhr frau- en so schö- -ne? So
En- gel hel- -le: "Bas su- chet jhr frau- en so schö- -ne? So
En- gel hel- -le: "Bas su- chet jhr frau- en so schö- -ne? So
En- gel hel- -le: "Bas su- chet jhr frau- en so schö- -ne? So

50
ist er ye er- -stan- -den, Den jhr da bol- tet sal-
ist er ye er- -stan- -den, Den jhr da bol- tet sal-
ist er ye er- -stan- -den, Den jhr da bol- tet sal-
ist er ye er- -stan- -den, Den jhr da bol- tet sal-

55
-ben." Ky-ri- e e-lei- -son. Al- -le- -lu-
-ben." Ky-ri- e e- lei- -son. Al- -le- -lu-
-ben." Ky-ri- e e- lei- -son. Al- le- lu- ia, Al- -le- -lu-
-ben." Ky- ri- e e- lei- -son. Al- -le- -lu-

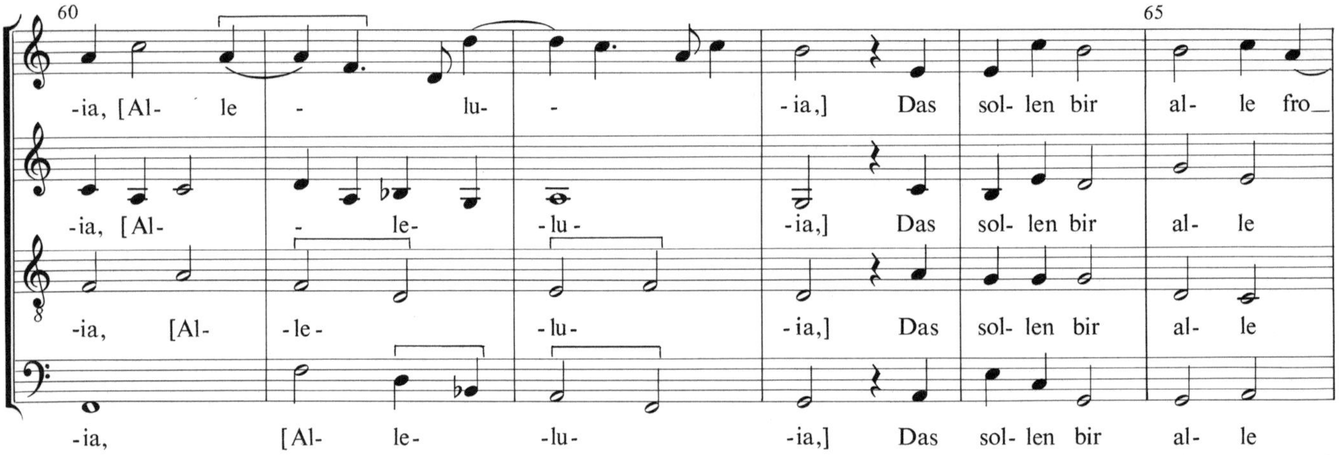

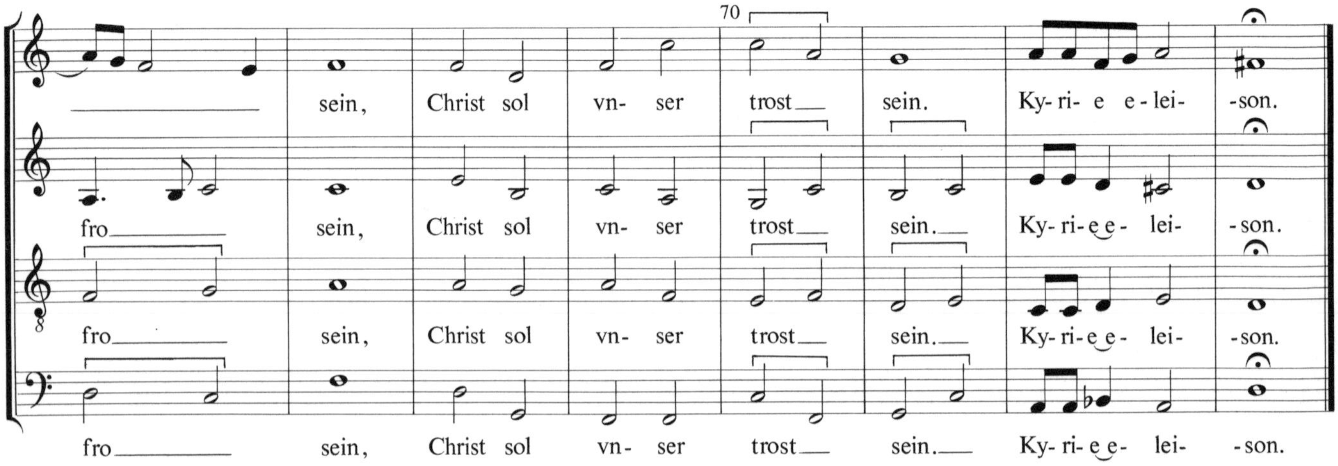

60
65
-ia, [Al- le - lu- - - ia,] Das sol- len bir al- le fro
-ia, [Al- - le- - lu - - ia,] Das sol- len bir al- le
-ia, [Al- - le - - lu- - ia,] Das sol- len bir al- le
-ia, [Al- le- - lu- - ia,] Das sol- len bir al- le

70
sein, Christ sol vn- ser trost sein. Ky- ri- e e - lei- -son.
fro sein, Christ sol vn- ser trost sein. Ky- ri- e e - lei- - son.
fro sein, Christ sol vn- ser trost sein. Ky- ri- e e - lei- - son.
fro sein, Christ sol vn- ser trost sein. Ky- ri- e e- lei- - son.

[6] Mitten wir im leben sind

Bartholomaeus Gesius
(ca. 1555-1613)

[CANTUS]
[ALTUS]
[TENOR]
[BASSUS]
5
Mit- ten wir im le- ben sind Mit dem todt vmb- fan-
Wen su- chen wir der hilf- fe thut Das wir gnad er- lan-
Mit- ten wir im le- - ben sind Mit dem todt vmb- fan-
Wen su- chen wir der hilf- - fe thut Das wir gnad er- lan-
Mit- ten wir im le- - ben sind Mit dem todt vmb- fan-
Wen su- chen wir der hilf- - fe thut Das wir gnad er- lan-
Mit- ten wir im le- - ben sind Mit dem todt vmb- fan-
Wen su- chen wir der hilf- - fe thut Das wir gnad er- lan-

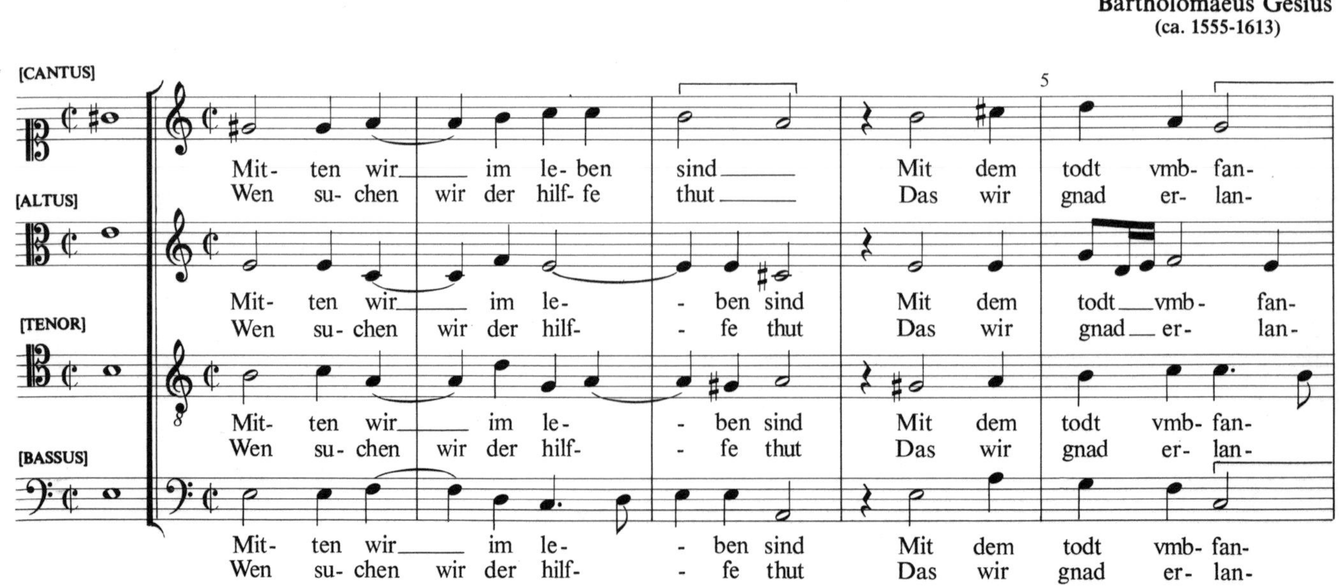

10
- gen: Das bis- tu, Herr, al- lei- - ne.
- gen?
- - gen: Das bis- tu, Herr, al- lei- - ne.
- - gen?
- - gen: Das bis- tu, Herr, al- lei- - ne.
- - gen?
- -gen: Das bis- tu, Herr, al- lei- - ne.
- -gen?

15
Vns re- -wet vn- ser mis- se- that, Die dich, Herr Gott, er-
Vns re- -wet vn- ser mis- se- -that, Die dich, Herr Gott, er-
Vns re- -wet vn- ser mis- se- -that, Die dich, Herr Gott, er-
Vns re- -wet vn- ser mis- se- -that, Die dich, Herr Gott, er-

20
-zür- net hat. Hei- li- - ger Her- re Gott, Hei- - li- ger
-zür- net hat. Hei- li- - ger Her- re Gott, Hei- - li- ger
-zür- net hat. Hei- li- - ger Her- re Gott, Hei- - li- ger
-zür- net hat. Hei- li- - ger Her- re Gott, Hei- - li- ger

25
star- cker Gott, Hei- li- -ger Barm- her- -zi- ger Hei- -land, Du
star- cker Gott, Hei- li- -ger Barm- her- -zi- ger Hei- -land, Du
star- cker Gott, Hei- li- -ger Barm- her- -zi- ger Hei- -land, Du
star- cker Gott, Hei- li- -ger Barm- her- -zi- ger Hei- -land, Du

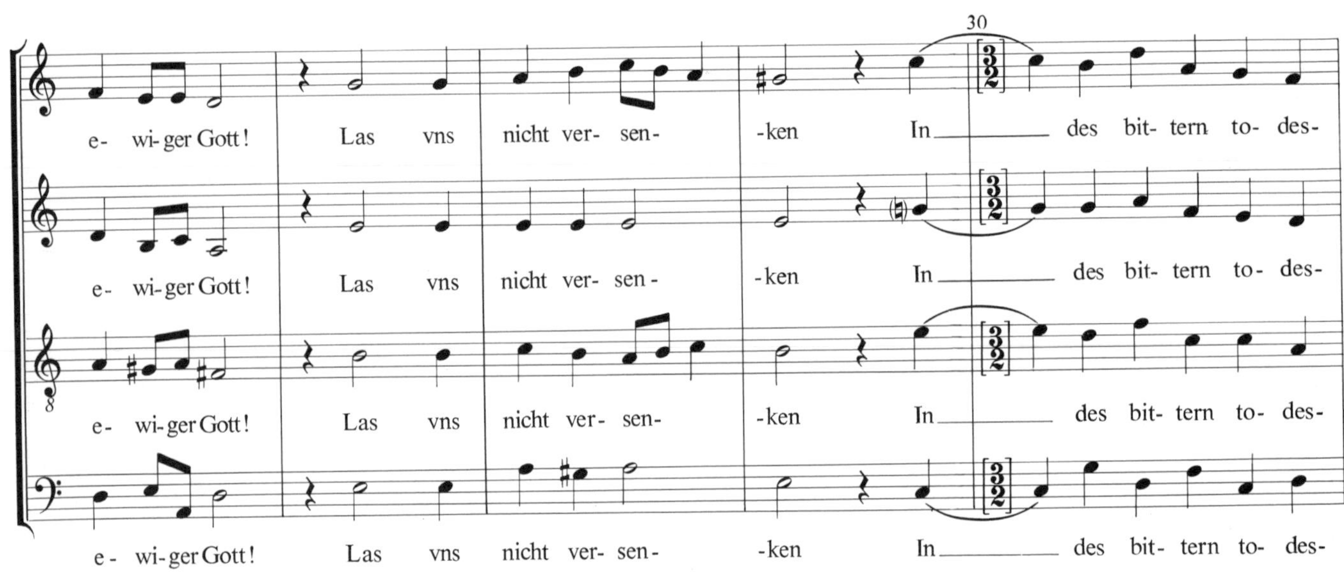
30
e- wi- ger Gott! Las vns nicht ver- sen- -ken In des bit- tern to- des-
e- wi- ger Gott! Las vns nicht ver- sen- -ken In des bit- tern to- des-
e- wi- ger Gott! Las vns nicht ver- sen- -ken In des bit- tern to- des-
e- wi- ger Gott! Las vns nicht ver- sen- -ken In des bit- tern to- des-

35
-noth! Ky- - ri- e e- - le- i- -son.
-noth! Ky- - ri- e e- - le- - i- - son.
-noth! Ky- - ri- e e- -le - i- - son.
-noth! Ky- - ri- e e- -le- - i- son.

[7] Gott sey gelobet vnd gebenedeiet

Sigmund Hemmel
(d. 1564)

15
vnd mit sei- nem blue- -te. Das gib vns Her- - re Gott
flei- sche vnd mit sei- nem blue- -te. Das gib
sei- nem flei- sche vnd mit sei- nem blue- te. Das gib vns
mit sei- nem blue- te, mit sei- nem blue- te. Das gib vns Herr

20
zu gue- - -te, Ky- ri- e- - -lei-
vns Herr zu gue- -te, Ky- ri- e- -lei-
Herr Gott zu gue- -te, Ky- - ri- e- -lei-
Gott zu gue- - -te, Ky- - ri- e e- -lei-

25
-son. Herr durch dei- nen hei- li- gen leich- - nam, Der
-son. Herr durch dei- nen hei- li- gen
-son. Herr durch dei- nen hei- li- gen leich- - nam, Der von
-son. Herr durch dei- nen heil- gen leich- nam, [heil- - gen leich-

30
35
von dei- ner muet- ter Ma- ri- a kam,
leich- nam, Der von dei- ner muet- ter Ma- -ri- a
dei- ner muet- ter, muet- ter Ma- -ri- a kam,
-nam,] Der von dei- ner muet- ter Ma- -ri- a kam

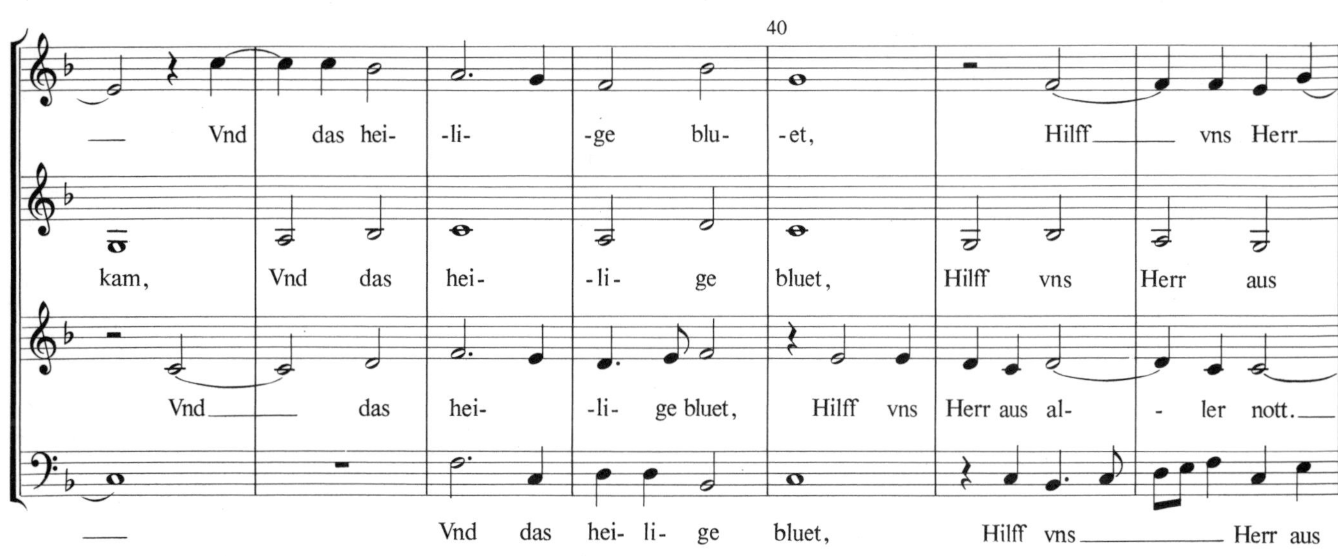
40
Vnd das hei- -li- -ge blu- -et, Hilff vns Herr
kam, Vnd das hei- -li- ge bluet, Hilff vns Herr aus
Vnd das hei- -li- ge bluet, Hilff vns Herr aus al- ler nott.
Vnd das hei- li- ge bluet, Hilff vns Herr aus

45
aus al- ler nott. Ky- ri- e- -lei- -son.
al- ler nott. Ky- ri- e- -lei- -son.
Ky- ri- e- lei- -son.
al- ler nott. Ky- ri- e- -lei- -son.

[8] Gelobet seistu Jesu Christ

Andreas Raselius
(1562–1602)

10
ei- ner Jung- frau das ist war, das ist war, Dess fre- wet
ei- ner Jung- -frau das ist war, das ist war, Dess fre- wet sich, Dess
ei- ner Jung- frau das ist war, das ist war, Dess fre- wet sich, Dess
ei- ner Jung- frau das ist war, Dess fre- wet
ei- ner Jung- frau das ist war, das ist war, Dess fre- wet sich, Dess

15
sich, Dess fre- wet sich der En- gel schar. Ky- ri- -e e- lei- son.
fre- wet sich, Dess fre- wet sich der En- gel schar. Ky- ri- -e e- lei- son.
fre- wet sich, Dess fre- wet sich der En-gel schar. Ky- ri- -e e- lei- son.
sich der En- gel schar. Ky- rie- -lei- son.
fre- wet sich, Dess fre- wet sich der En- gel schar. Ky- ri- -e e- lei- son.

[9] Nun bitten wir den heiligen Geist

Johannes Rasch
(1540–1612)

-ten glau- ben al- - ler- - meist, Dass
al- - ler- meist, Dass er vns be- -hü- - te an
- ler- meist, Dass er vns be-hü- - te an vn- serm en-
-ben al- - ler- -meist, Dass er vns be- hü- -te an vn- serm
-ben al- -ler- meist, Dass er vns be- hü-
er vns be- -hü- te an vn-serm en- de, wenn wir heim-farn aus
vn- serm en- -de, wenn wir heim- farn aus di- sem
- de, wenn wir heim- farn, heim- farn aus
en- de, an vn- serm en- de, wenn wir heim- -farn aus di- sem
-te an vn- serm en- de, wenn wir heim- -farn aus
di- sem e- len- -de. Ky- - ri- e e- lei- - son.]
e- len- de. Ky- - ri- -e e- -lei- - son.]
di- sem e- -le- de. Ky- - ri- e e- - lei- - son.]
e- len- de. Ky- ri- -e e- - lei- - son.]
di- sem e- len- de. Ky- ri- e- -lei- -son.

[10] Gott sey gelobet vnd gebenedeiet

Balduin Hoyoul
(1547–1652)

10
hat ge- spei- -set, [Der vns sel- ber hat ge- spei- set] Mit sei- nem
-set, Der vns sel- -ber hat ge- spei- - set Mit sei- nem
Der vns sel- -ber hat ge- spei- -set Mit sei- nem
vns sel- - ber hat ge- -spei- set
-set, Der vns sel- -ber hat ge- spei- -set Mit

15
flei- sche vnd mit sei- - nem blü- -te, [Mit sei- - nem blü-
flei- sche, Mit sei- nem flei- -sche vnd mit sei- -nem blü- te.
flei- -sche, Mit sei- nem flei- -sche vnd mit sei- -nem blü- te. Das
Mit sei- nem flei- -sche vnd mit sei- nem blü- te.
sei- nem flei- sche vnd mit sei- -nem blü- te.

20
-te.] Das gib vns Herr Gott zu gü- -te, Das gib
Das gib vns Herr Gott zu gü- -te, Das gib vns
gib vns Herr Gott zu gü- te, Das gib vns
Das gib vns Herr
Das gib vns Herr Gott zu gü- te, Das gib vns

25
30
vns Herr Gott zu gü- te, Ky- ri- -e e- lei- -son. Herr durch
Herr Gott zu gü- - te, Ky- - ri- e e- lei- -son. Herr durch
Herr Gott zu gü- -te, Ky- - ri- e e- lei- - son. Herr durch dei-
Gott zu gü- te, Ky- ri- e e- lei- -son.
Herr Gott zu gü- te, Ky- - ri- e e- -lei- - son. Herr durch

35
dei- nen hei- -li- gen leich- -nam, Der von dei- ner
dei- nen hei- - - li- -gen leich- nam, Der von
- nen hei- - li- gen leich- nam, [Herr durch dei- -nen hei- li- gen leich- nam,]
Herr durch dei- -nen hei- - li- gen leich- nam, Der
dei- nen hei- - li- gen leich- -nam, Der von

40
Müt- ter Ma- - ri- a kam, Vnd das hei- li- ge
dei- ner Müt- -ter Ma- ri- - - a kam,Vnd das hei- li- ge
Der von dei- ner Müt- ter Ma- - ri- a kam,Vnd das hei- li- ge
von dei- -ner Müt- - ter Ma- -ri- a kam,
dei- ner Müt- -ter Ma- - ri- - a kam, Vnd das hei- li- ge

45
blüt, [Vnd das hei- li- ge blüt,] Hilff vns herr auss al- -ler not, [Hilff
blüt, Vnd das hei- li- ge blüt, Hilff vns herr auss al- ler not, [Hilff
blüt, [Vnd das hei- -li- ge blüt,] Hilff vns herr auss al- ler not, Hilff vns
Vnd das hei- li- -ge blüt, Hilff vns
blüt, [Vnd das hei- li- -ge blüt,] Hilff vns herr auss al- ler not, Hilff

50
vns herr auss al- ler not.] Ky- -ri- e e- lei- -son.
vns herr auss al- - ler not.] Ky- - ri- e e- lei- -son.
herr auss al- -ler not. Ky- - ri- e e- lei- -son.
herr auss al- ler not. Ky- ri- e e- lei- son.
vns herr auss al- -ler not. Ky- -ri- e e- -lei- -son.

[11] Christ lag in Todesbanden

Ludwig Daser
(1525–1589)

10
-ge- ben. Der ist wie- der
- ben, Für vn- ser sünd ge- -ge- ben. Der ist wie-
- ben. Der ist wie- der er- stan- -den, Der ist wie- der
Für vn- -ser sünd ge- ge- -ben.
-ben, Für vn- -ser sünd ge- ge- - ben. Der ist wie- der er-

15
er- stan- - den Vnd hat
-der er- -stan- den, Der ist wie- -der er- stan- -den Vnd
er- - stan- den, Der ist wie- -der er- stan- -den Vnd
Der ist wie- -der er- -stan- -den
-stan- - den, Der ist wie- -der er- stan- -den Vnd hat vns

20
vns bracht das le- -ben.
hat vns bracht das le- -ben, Vnd hat vns bracht das
hat vns bracht das le- ben, Vnd hat vns bracht das
Vnd hat vns bracht das
bracht das le- ben, Vnd hat vns bracht das le-

25
Das wir sol- -len frö- -lich sein:
le- ben. Das wir sol- - len frö- - lich sein, Das wir sol- len
le- ben. Das wir sol- len frö- lich sein, Das wir sol-
le - ben. Das wir sol- len
-ben. Das wir sol- - len frö- lich sein, [frö- lich sein, Das wir

30
Gott lo- -ben vnd danck- -bar sein.
frö- lich sein: Gott lo- -ben vnd danck- bar sein, Gott lo-
- len frö- lich sein: Gott lo- - ben vnd danck- -bar sein, [Gott lo- ben
frö- lich sein: Gott lo - ben vnd
sol- len frö- lich sein:] Gott lo- ben vnd danck- bar sein, Gott lo-

35
Vnd sin- -gen Al- -le- lu- - ia,
-ben vnd danck-bar sein. Vnd sin- gen Al- - le- lu- - ia, Vnd
vnd danck- bar sein.] Vnd sin- gen Al- le- - lu- ia,
danck- bar sein. Vnd
-ben vnd danck- bar sein. Vnd sin- gen Al- - le- lu- - ia,

Al- le- lu- -ia,
sin- -gen Al- le- - lu- -ia, Al- le- lu- -ia, [Al- le- lu-
Vnd sin- - gen Al- -le- lu- -ia, Al- le- lu- -ia, [Al- le- lu-
sin- gen Al- le- -lu- -ia, Al- le- lu-
Vnd sin- -gen Al- le- -lu- -ia, Al- le- lu- -ia, Al- le- lu-

[Al- le- lu- -ia,] Al- - le- lu- -ia, [Al- - le- lu- - ia!]
-ia, Al- le- lu- -ia, Al- le- - lu- -ia!]
-ia, Al- le- lu- -ia,] Al- le- lu- -ia, Al- - le- lu- -ia!
-ia, Al- le- -lu- -ia!
-ia, [Al- le- lu- -ia,] Al- le- lu- -ia, Al- - le- lu- ia!

[12] Christus surrexit

Anonymous

te- -xit, te- - - -
- xit, te- - -xit, et quos hic
te- [xit,] te- - -
-la no - -stra te- - xit, et
-xit, te- - -xit,
et quos hic di- -le-

- - - - - - xit, et
di- -le- xit nos ad
- - - xit et quos hic di- -le- -xit, di-
quos hic di- -le- -xit, di- -le-
et quos di- -le- -xit
-xit, di- -le- - -xit, di- -le-

35

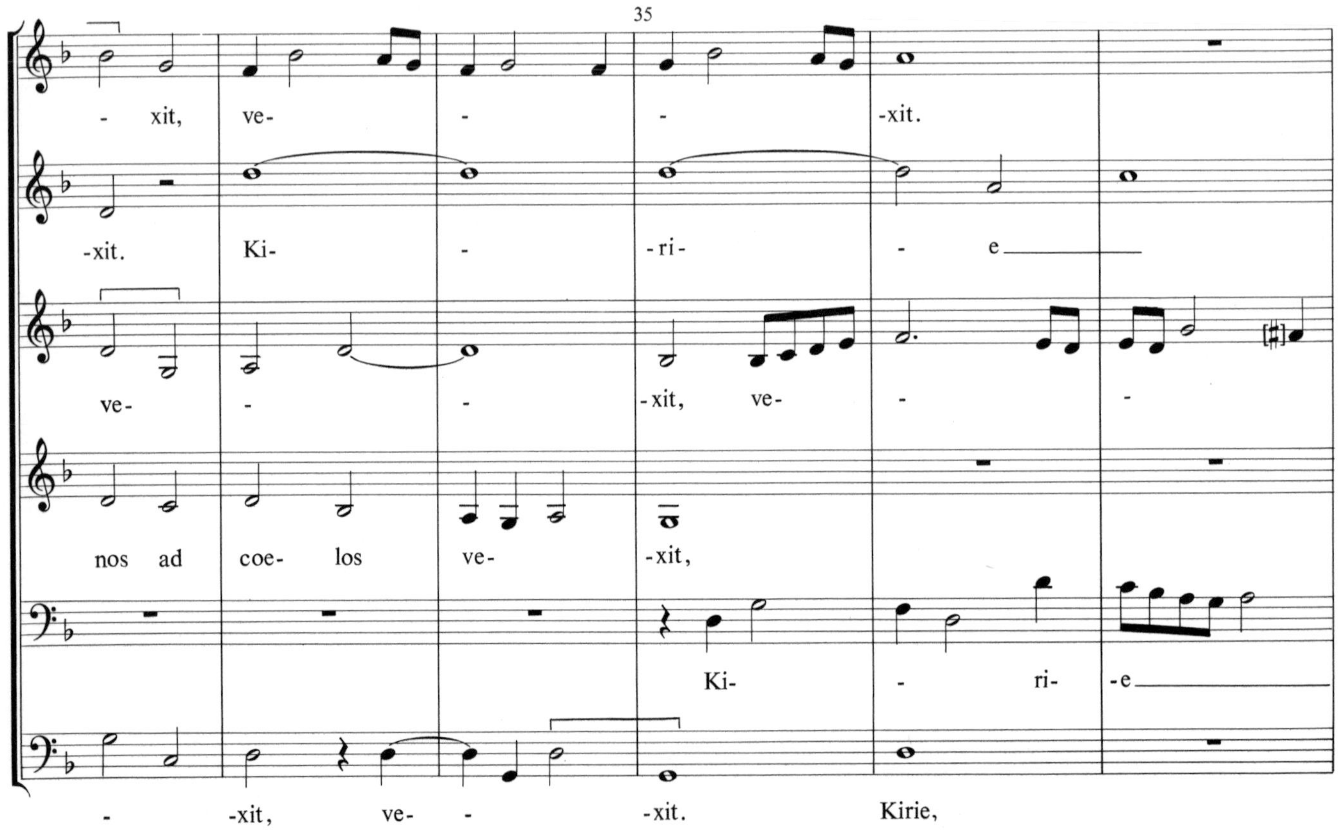

- xit, ve- - - -xit.

-xit. Ki- - -ri- - e

ve- - - -xit, ve- - -

nos ad coe- los ve- -xit,

Ki- - ri- -e

- -xit, ve- - -xit. Kirie,

[13] Christ ist erstanden

Anonymous

10
von der mar- -ter al- - - le,
- -den von der mar- ter al-
der mar- - ter al- - le, von
- -den
-den von der mar- - ter
-stan- -den Christ ist

15
al- - - - -le,
- - - - - -le,
der mar- -ter al- - -le, al- -
von der mar- -ter al- - le,
al- -le, von der mar- ter
er- stan- - den von der

20
des sol wir al- le fro
des sol wir al- le fro sein,
- - le,
al- - - -le,
al- - le, des sol wir al- -le fro
mar- ter al- -le, al-

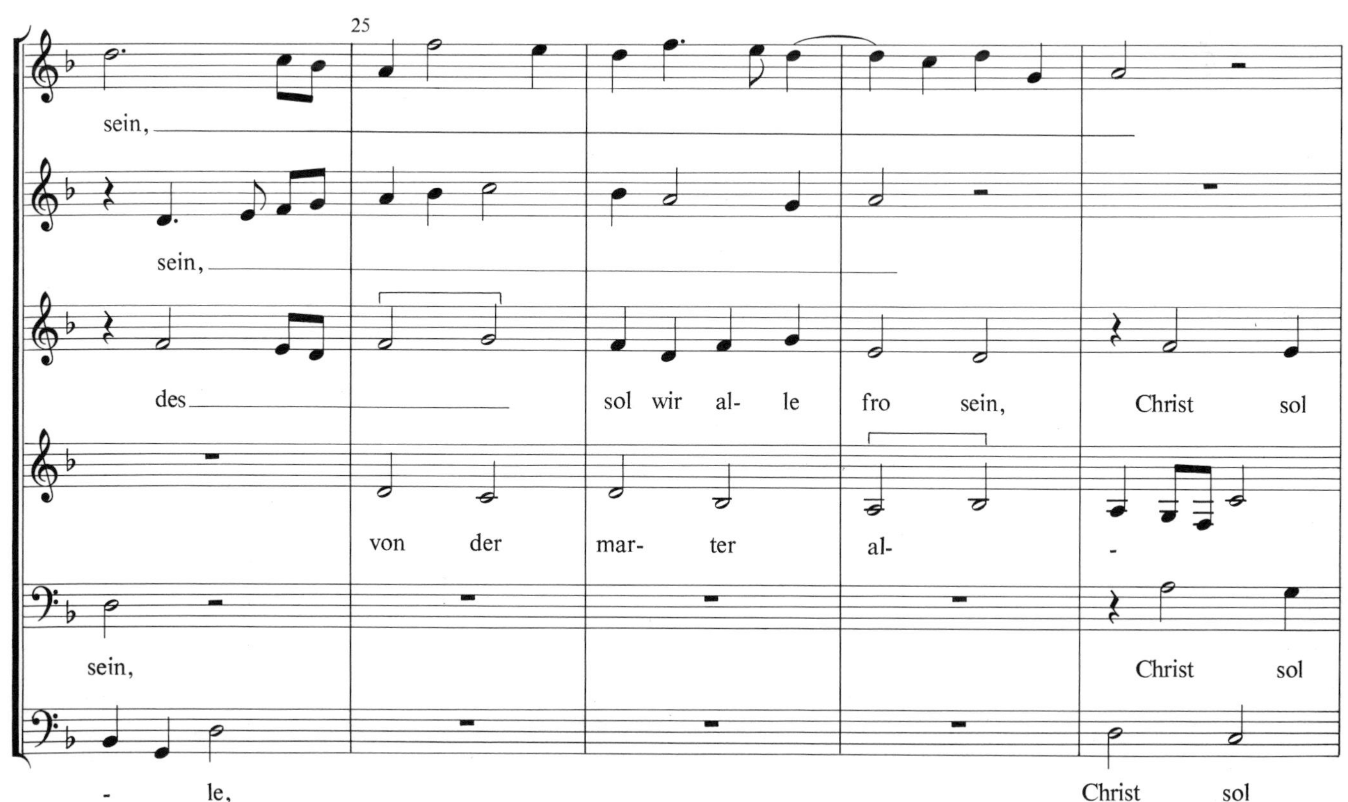
25
sein,
sein,
des sol wir al- le fro sein, Christ sol
von der mar- ter al- -
sein, Christ sol
- le, Christ sol

30
Christ sol vn- ser trost
Christ sol vn- ser trost
vn- ser trost sein.
- - -le, Christ sol vn-
vn- ser trost sein, sein.
vn- ser trost sein.

35
40
sein. Ky- -ri- e, Ky- -ri- e e- - lei- -son.
sein. Ky- ri- -e, Kyrielei- -son.
Ky- -ri- e- lei- -son, Ky- - ri- e- -lei- -son.
-ser trost sein. Ky- ri- e- -lei- - -son.
Ky- ri- -e, Ky- -ri- e, Ky- ri- e- - lei- -son.
Ky- ri- e- -lei- son, Ky- ri- e- -lei- - son, lei- -son.

[14] Jesus Christus vero est agnus
Jesus Christus Vnser Heiland / Gratia sit Deo
Christ ist erstanden

Anonymous

15
[ve- ro est a - - gnus,] ve- ro est a - gnus,
- -stus Vn- ser Hei- land, der
- gnus, ve- -ro est a - gnus, qui ab-
Chri - -stus ve- - ro est a - gnus, qui ab-
ve- -ro est a -
- gnus, [ve- -ro est a - - gnus,] qui ab-

20
qui ab- - vit pec- ca- -ta mun- -di, pec- ca- ta
den todt v- -ber- wandt, ist auff-
-vit, [qui ab- vit] pec- ca- -ta, [pec- ca- -ta,] pec-
- -vit pec- -ca- ta, pec- - ca- ta mun- di,
-gnus, qui ab- -vit pec- ca-
- vit, [qui ab- -vit] pec- ca- ta, pec- -ca- ta

25
mun- -di, qui ab- -vit pec- ca- - ta mun- - di,
-er- stan- - den. qui ab- vit
-ca- ta mun- - - -di, qui ab- - vit pec- ca-
pec- ca- ta mun- -di,
-ta mun- - -di, qui ab- - vit pec- ca- ta
mun- di, pec- -ca- ta mun- - di, qui ab- -vit pec- ca- ta

30
qui ab- - -vit pec- ca- -ta
pec- ca- - ta mun- - di,
-ta mun- - di, [qui ab- -vit pec- ca- ta mun-
qui ab- vit pec- -ca-
mun- -di, pec- ca- -ta mun- -di,
mun- di, qui ab- - vit pec- ca- ta mun- di, qui

35
mun- - - di,
Die sünd hat er
-di,] pec- ca- -ta mun- - -di, pec- -ca-
-ta mun- - - di, qui mor- tem mo- -rien- do de -
ab- vit pec- -ca- ta mun- - di, qui mor- tem mo-

40
qui mor- tem mo- rien- - do de - - stru- xit,
ge- fan- - gen. Ky- ri-
-ta, qui mor- tem mo- -rien- do de - -
-stru- - -xit, qui mor- tem
qui mor- -tem mo- -ri- en-
- -rien- do de - - stru- xit,

45
[qui mor-tem mo- rien- -do de - stru- xit,] mo- -rien- do de - - stru- xit.
-e- lei- -son. Ky- -ri- e, Ky- ri-
- stru- xit, [qui mor- tem mo- -rien- do de - stru- xit,
mo- rien- - do de - -stru- - -
-do de - - stru- - xit.
qui mor- tem mo- rien- -do de - stru- xit.

50
Ky- ri- e- - lei- -son,
-e.
Die sünd hat er ge- fan- gen.
qui mor- tem mo- ri- - en- - do de - - stru-
-xit. Ky- - ri- e- - lei- -son, vi- tam, vi-
et vi- - - tam
Ky- ri- e- -lei- son, Ky- -ri- e- lei- - son, et vi-

55
et vi- -
Ky- ri- - e e- -lei- son,
-xit, mo- - ri- -en- do de- stru- - xit, [mor-
-tam re- sur- -gen- do re- pa- - ra- vit, et vi-
re- sur- - gen- -do re- -pa- -ra- vit,
- tam re- sur- gen- -do re- pa- - ra- vit, et

60
-tam re- sur- -gen- -do re- - pa-
[Ky- ri- - e- - lei- son,] Ky- ri- e- -lei- son,
- tem, mo- -rien- do de - stru- - xit.] Al- le-
- tam re- - sur- gen- - do re- -pa- ra- -vit, re-
vi- - - tam re- - sur- gen- - do

-ra- vit. Al- - le- lu- ia, [Al-
[Ky- ri- - e
-lu- ia, [Al- le- -lu- ia, Al- -
- pa- ra- -vit. Al- le- - - lu- - ia,
et vi- -tam re- -sur- -gen-
re- -pa- -ra- - vit. Al-

- le- lu- -ia, Al- le- lu- -ia,] Al- - le- - lu- -ia.
e- lei- - son, Ky- ri- -e e- le- i- - son.]
-le- lu- -ia,] Al- le- -lu- ia, Al- -le- lu- -ia.
[Al- - le- lu- ia, Al- le- lu- -ia, Al- -le- lu- -ia.]
-do re- pa- - ra- -vit, re- pa- - ra- -vit.
- le- lu- ia, [Al- le- lu- -ia, Al- le- lu- -ia,] Al- -le- lu- -ia.

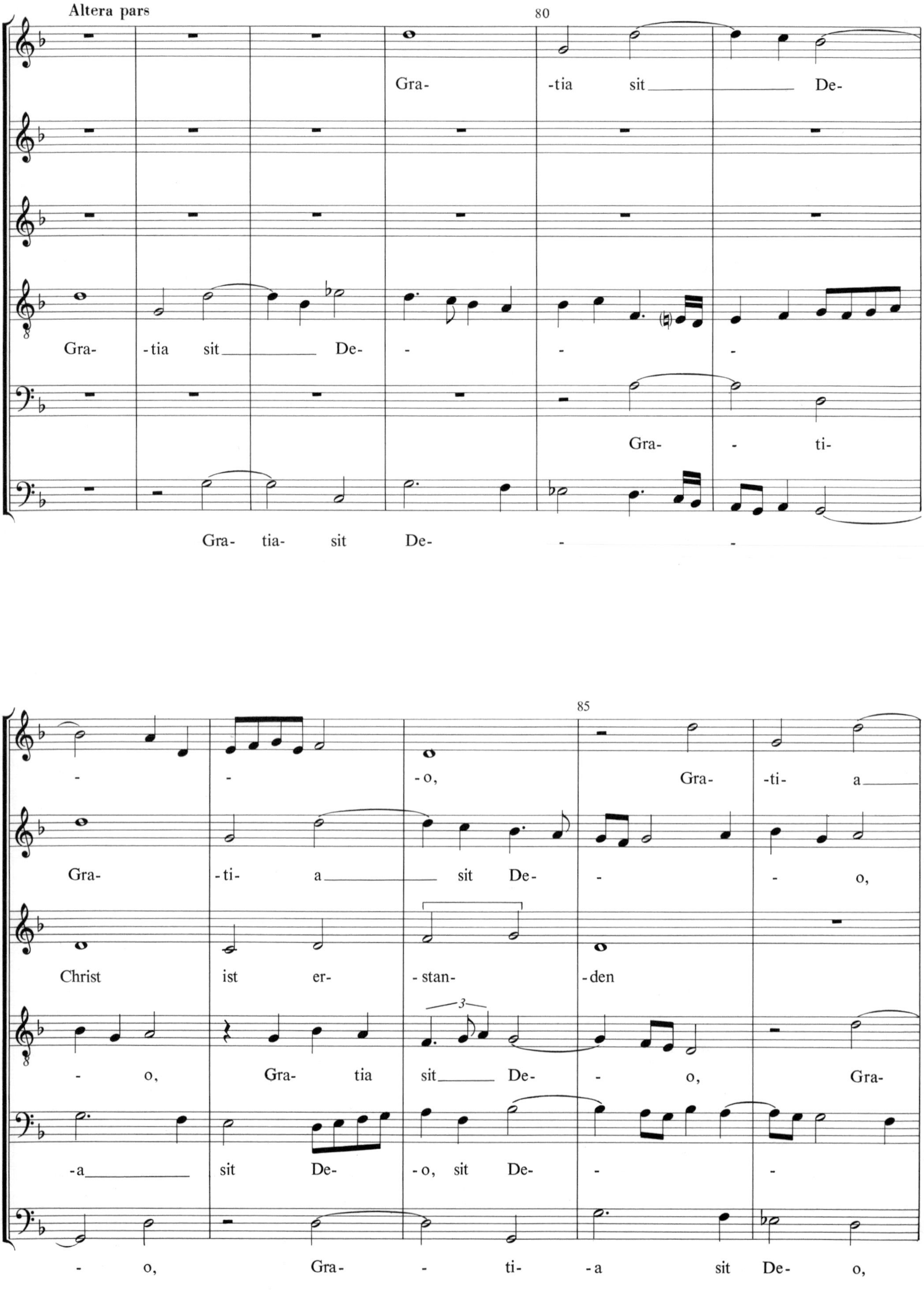

85

- - -o, Gra- -ti- a

Gra- -ti- a sit De- - - o,

Christ ist er- -stan- -den

- o, Gra- tia sit De- - o, Gra-

-a sit De- -o, sit De- - -

- o, Gra- - ti- -a sit De- o,

90
sit De- - o
sit De- - -o qui de- -dit no- bis
Von der Mar-
- tia sit De- - -o qui de- dit
- -o, Gra- tia sit De- - o
[Gra- -ti- a sit De- -o] qui

95
qui de- -dit no- bis vic- - to-
vic- to- - ri- -am, qui de- dit no- -bis vic- to-
-ter al- - len,
no- bis vic- - to- ri- -am, [qui de- dit no- bis vic-
qui de- -dit no- bis vic- -to- ri- am, [qui de-
de- dit no- -bis vic- -to- ri- am, [qui de- -dit no- bis vic-

100
- - ri- -am, qui de- -dit no- bis
- ri- am, vic- to- ri- -am, qui de- dit no- - bis vic-
-to- ri- am,] qui de- -dit no- -bis vic- -to- ri- am
-dit no- -bis vic- to- ri- am,]
-to- ri- am,] qui de- -dit no-

105
vic- to- ri- -am per Je-
- to- ri- -am per Je- sum Chri- stum Do- mi- -num no- strum,
Des sol- len wir al- -le froh
per Je- -sum Chri - stum Do- - - mi- num
qui de- -dit no- bis vic- to- ri- -am per Je- - sum Chri -
-bis vic- -to- ri- am per Je- sum

110
-sum Chri- - stum Do- - mi- num no- strum, [per Je- sum
per Je- sum Chri- -stum Do- mi-
sein, Christ wil
no- -strum, per Je- sum Chri- -
- stum Do- mi- -num no- -strum, per Je- sum Chri- - stum,
Chri - stum Do- -mi- num, Chri - stum Do-

115
Chri- stum Do- - mi- num no - -strum,] per Je- -sum Chri - stum
- num no-strum, per Je- sum Chri- stum Do- mi-
vn- ser trost sein. Ky- ri- - e- leis.
- stum Do- - mi- num no - - strum, per Je- sum
[per Je- sum Chri - stum] Do- -mi- num no- -strum
- - mi- num, per Je- sum Chri - stum Do- -mi- num

120
Do- mi- - num no- strum, Do- mi- -num no- strum,
-num no- -strum, Do- mi- -num no- strum,
per Je- sum Chri- - stum
Chri- stum [Do- - - mi- - num no - -strum,] Do-
per Je- -sum Chri- -stum, Do- - mi- num no- strum,
no- strum, per Je- sum Chri- stum Do- - mi- num

125
[Do- mi- num no- strum,] A- - men.
Do- mi-num no- strum, A- - - - men.
Do- mi- num no- strum, A- - men.
- mi- num no- strum, Do- - mi- num no - - -strum.
no- -strum, A- men, A- - - - men.
no - - strum, A- - - men.

[15] Nun bitten wir den heiligen Geist

Anonymous

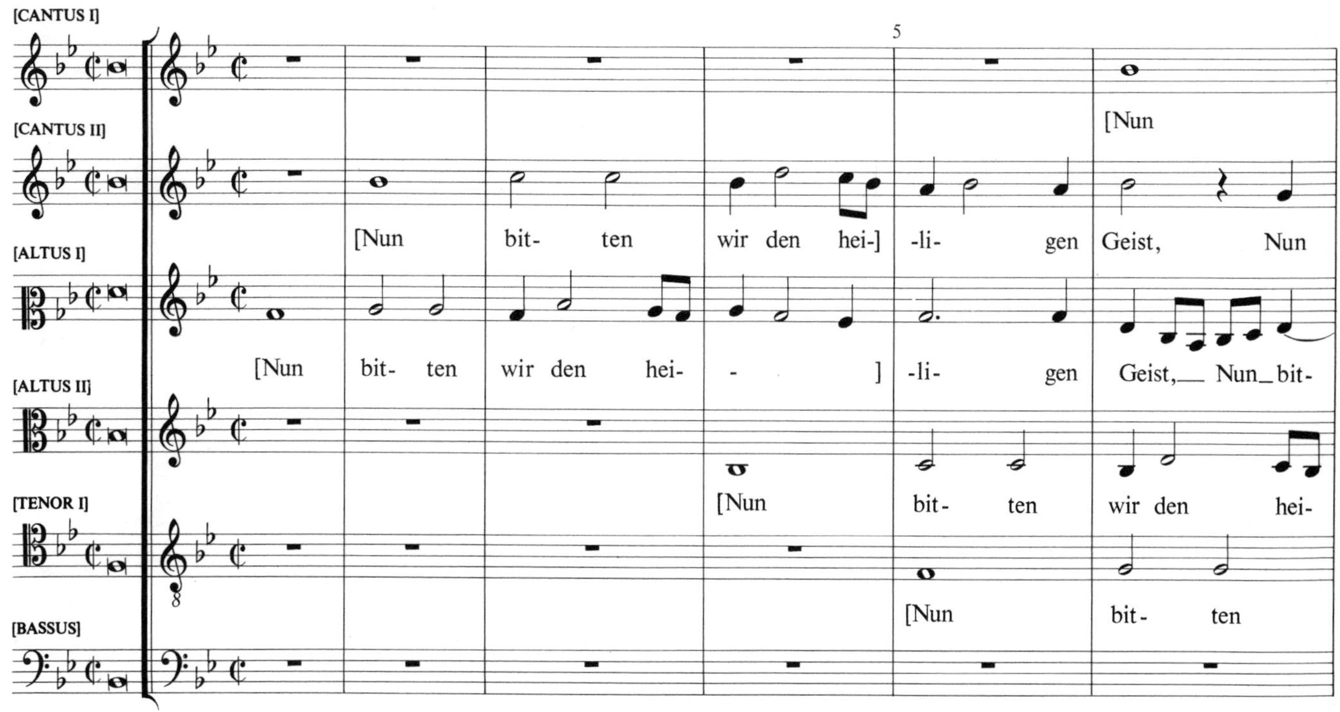

15
Geist Vmb den rech- ten glau- ben, glau- - ben al-
den rech- - ten, Vmb den rech- -ten glau- -
Geist, hei- li- gen Geist Vmb den rech- ten glau- ben,
Geist Vmb den rech- - ten glau- -ben, glau-
hei- li- gen Geist Vmb den rech- ten glau- - ben
-li- gen Geist Vmb den rech- ten glau- -ben al-

20
-ler- -meist, al- - ler- meist,
- ben al- - - ler- - meist, Das
glau- -ben al- - ler- meist, Das
- -ben al- - - ler- meist,
al- ler- -meist, al- - - ler- meist, Das
- ler- -meist, [al- - - ler- meist,]

Das ehr vns be- - hü- -te, be- hü-
ehr vns, Das ehr vns be- -hü-
ehr vns be- -hü- -te, be- -hü-
Das ehr vns be- -hü-
ehr vns be- - hü- - te,
Das ehr vns be- -hü-

25
- te, be- hü- -te, be- - hü-
- -te, Das ehr vns be- -hü- te,
-te, Das ehr vns be- -
-te, Das ehr vns be- hü- -
Das ehr vns be- - hü- -
-te,

30
-te an vn- serm En- -de, an vn- serm En-
Das ehr vns be- -hü- te an vn- serm
-hü- - -te an vn- serm
- - -te an vn- serm
- -te an vn- serm En- de, vn- serm, vn- serm
be- - hü- -te an vn- serm

35
- de, Wenn wir heim- -
En- -de, Wenn wir heim-
En- -de, Wenn wir heim-
En- - -de, Wenn wir
En- de, Wenn wir heim- fa-
En- - -de, Wenn wir

40
-fa- ren aus die- sem, aus die- sem E- -
-fa- -ren aus die- sem E- -lende,
- -fa- -ren aus die- sem E- -len- de,
heim- - -faren aus
- ren aus die- sem E- len- -de, aus
heim- fa- - -ren aus die- sem E-

45
- len- -de. Ky- ri- e e- lei-
aus die- sem E- - len- de. Ky- - ri- e e-
aus die- sem E- -len- de. Ky- -ri- e e-
die- sem E- - len- -de. Ky- ri- e- -le- i- son, Ky- ri-
die- sem E- - len- -de, E- -len- de.
-len- de, aus die- sem E- -len- de. Ky- ri-

50
-son, e- -le- i- son, Ky- ri-
-lei- - -son.
-lei- son, e- -le- i- son, Ky- - ri- -e e- le-
-e e- -le- i- -son.
Ky- ri- -e e- le- i-
-e e- - le- i- -son, Ky- - ri- e e-

55
-e, Ky- ri- -e e- le- i- -son.
- i- son, Ky- - ri- -e e- - le- i- -son.
-son, Ky- ri- -e e- le- i- -son, Ky- ri- -e e- le- i- -son.
-le- - i- -son, e- le- i- son.

[16] Christ lag in Todesbanden

Christoph Thomas Walliser
(1568–1648)

-ban- den, in To- des- -ban- den, [in To- des- -ban-
-stan- den, wie- - der er- -stan- den, [wie-der er- -stan-

- den,] in To- des- ban- - den, [in To- des- -ban-
- den,] wie- -der er- stan- - den, [wie-der er- -stan-

- den, in To- -des- ban- - den, [in To- des- -ban-
- den, wie- der er- stan- - den, [wie-der er- -stan-

in To- -des, in To- des- -ban- den, [in To- des- ban-
wie- der, wie- der er- -stan- den, [wie- -der er- stan-

- den in To- des- - ban- -
- den wie- -der er- - stan- -

-den,] Für vn- ser Sünd, [Für vn- ser Sünd] ge-
-den] Vnd hat vns bracht, [Vnd hat vns bracht] das

-den,] Für vn- ser Sünd, [Für vn- ser Sünd,] Für vn- ser Sünd ge-
-den] Vnd hat vns bracht, [Vnd hat vns bracht,] Vnd hat vns bracht das

-den,] Für vn- ser Sünd, [Für vn- ser Sünd,] Für vn- ser Sünd ge-
-den] Vnd hat vns bracht, [Vnd hat vns bracht,] Vnd hat vns bracht das

-den,] Für vn- ser Sünd, [Für vn- ser Sünd] ge- ge-
-den] Vnd hat vns bracht, [Vnd hat vns bracht] das le-

-den, Für vn- ser Sünd, [Für vn- ser Sünd,]
-den Vnd hat vns bracht, [Vnd hat vns bracht,]

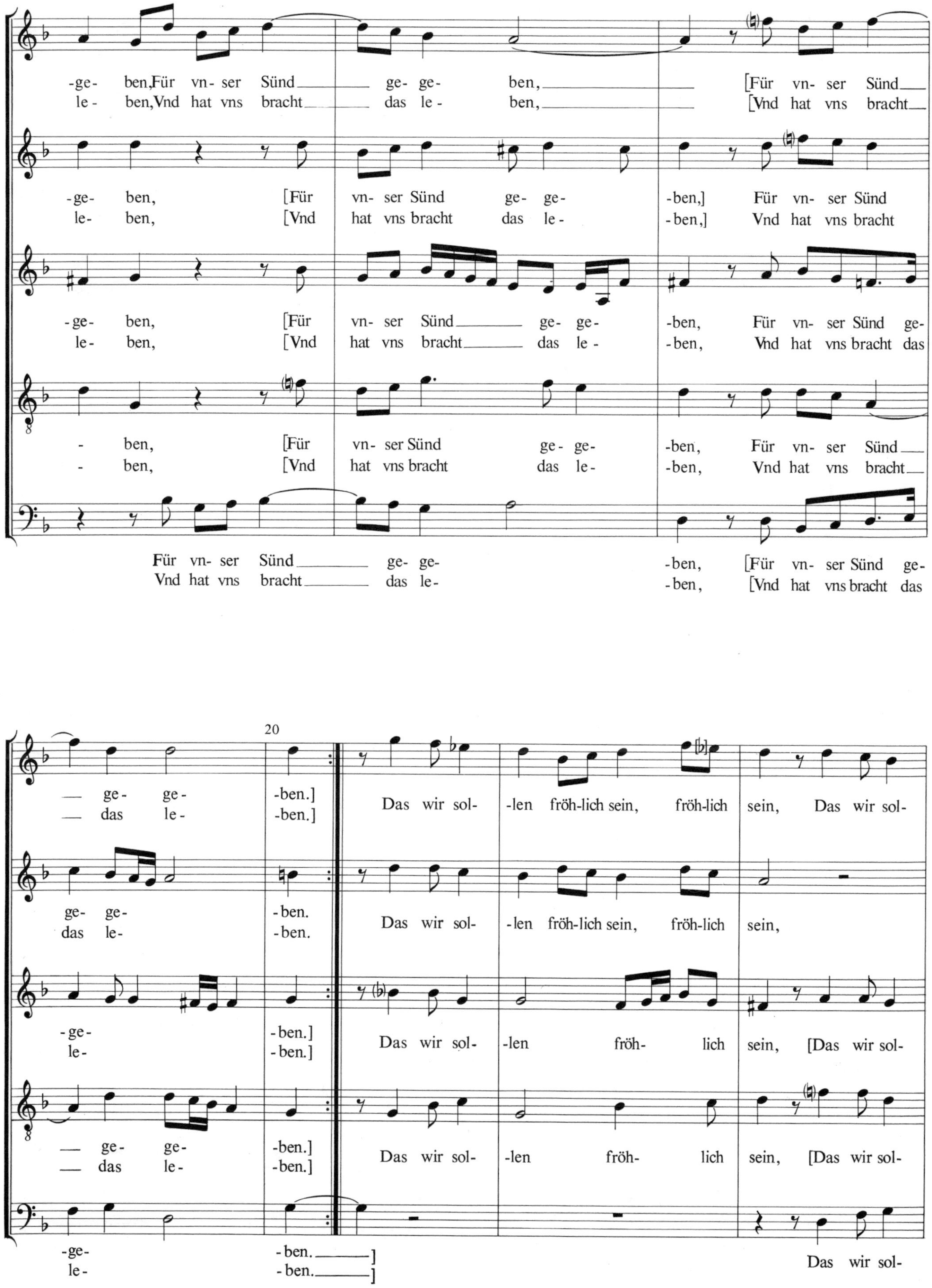

-ge- ben,Für vn- ser Sünd ge- ge- ben, [Für vn- ser Sünd
le- ben,Vnd hat vns bracht das le- ben, [Vnd hat vns bracht

-ge- ben, [Für vn- ser Sünd ge- ge- -ben,] Für vn- ser Sünd
le- ben, [Vnd hat vns bracht das le- -ben,] Vnd hat vns bracht

-ge- ben, [Für vn- ser Sünd ge- ge- -ben, Für vn- ser Sünd ge-
le- ben, [Vnd hat vns bracht das le- -ben, Vnd hat vns bracht das

- ben, [Für vn- ser Sünd ge- ge- -ben, Für vn- ser Sünd
- ben, [Vnd hat vns bracht das le- -ben, Vnd hat vns bracht

Für vn- ser Sünd ge- ge- -ben, [Für vn- ser Sünd ge-
Vnd hat vns bracht das le- -ben, [Vnd hat vns bracht das

20
ge- ge- -ben.] Das wir sol- -len fröh-lich sein, fröh-lich sein, Das wir sol-
das le- -ben.]
ge- ge- -ben. Das wir sol- -len fröh-lich sein, fröh-lich sein,
das le- -ben.
-ge- -ben.] Das wir sol- -len fröh- lich sein, [Das wir sol-
le- -ben.]
ge- ge- -ben.] Das wir sol- -len fröh- lich sein, [Das wir sol-
das le- -ben.]
-ge- -ben.] Das wir sol-
le- -ben.]

25
-len fröh- lich sein, fröh- lich sein: Gott lo- ben, [Gott lo-
fröh-lich sein, [fröh- lich sein:] Gott lo- ben, [Gott
-len] fröh- lich sein, fröh- - lich sein: Gott lo- ben, [Gott
-len fröh- lich sein, fröh- lich sein: Gott lo- ben,
-len fröh-lich sein, fröh- lich sein: Gott lo-

- ben, Gott lo- ben vnd danck- - bar sein, vnd
lo- ben, Gott lo- -ben vnd danck-bar sein,] vnd danck- bar
lo- ben] vnd danck- bar sein, [vnd danck- bar sein,] Gott lo- ben vnd
[Gott lo- ben] vnd danck-bar sein,] vnd danck- bar
-ben vnd danck- -bar sein, vnd

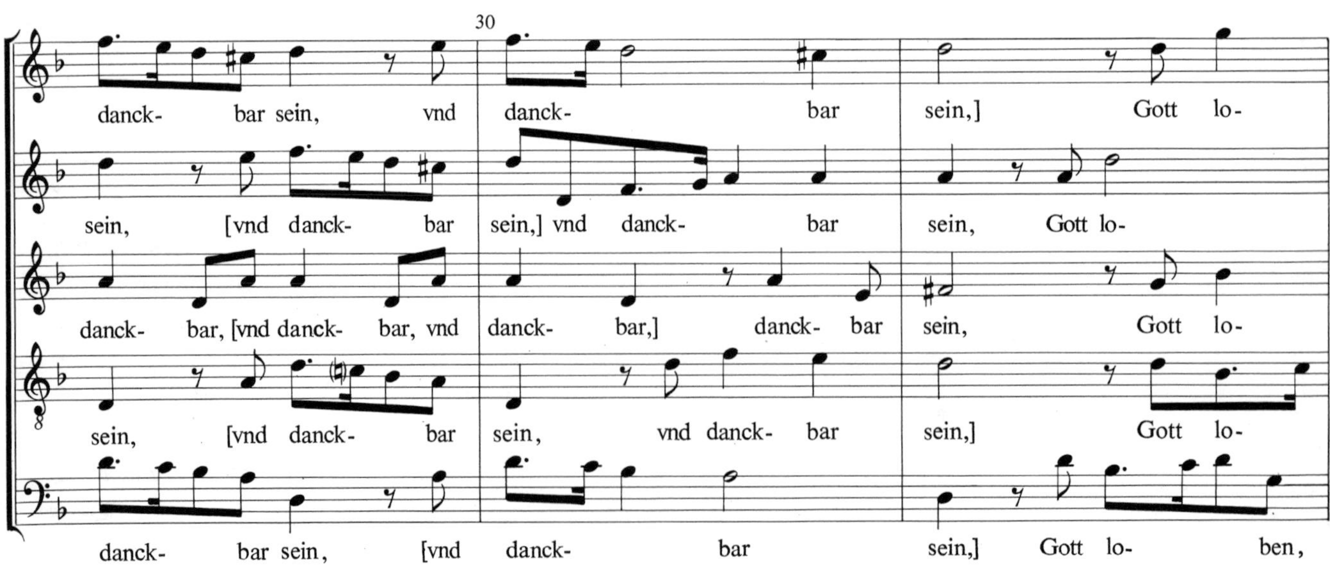
30
danck- bar sein, vnd danck- bar sein,] Gott lo-
sein, [vnd danck- bar sein,] vnd danck- bar sein, Gott lo-
danck- bar, [vnd danck- bar, vnd danck- bar,] danck- bar sein, Gott lo-
sein, [vnd danck- bar sein, vnd danck- bar sein,] Gott lo-
danck- bar sein, [vnd danck- bar sein,] Gott lo- ben,

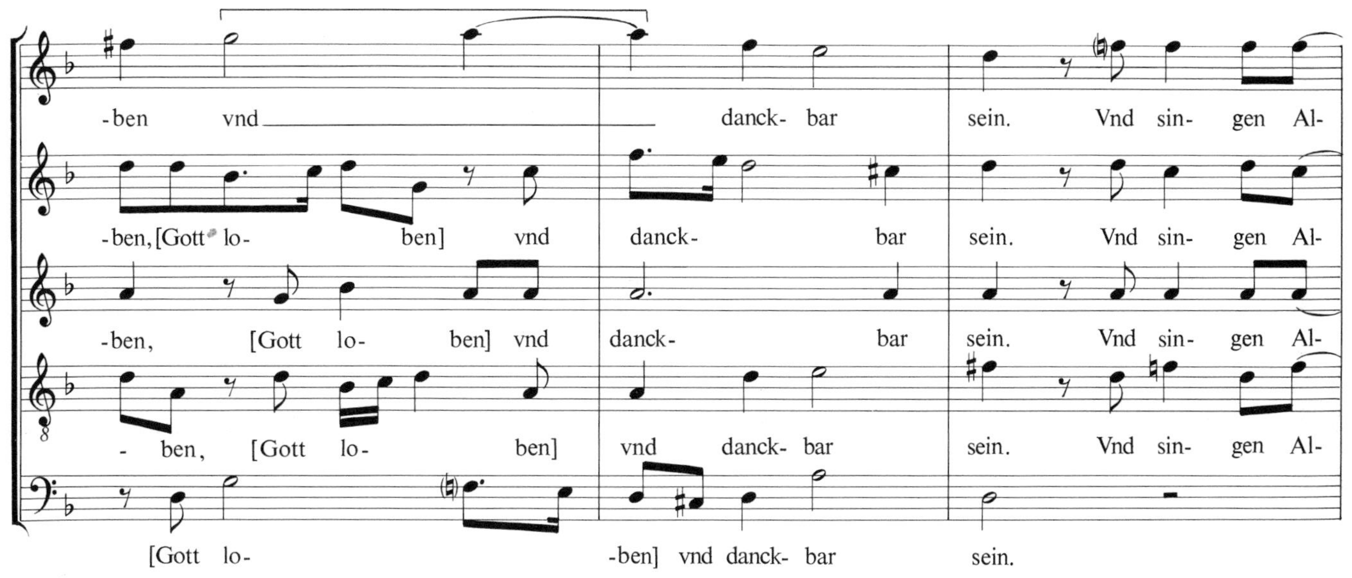
-ben vnd danck- bar sein. Vnd sin- gen Al-
-ben, [Gott lo- ben] vnd danck- bar sein. Vnd sin- gen Al-
-ben, [Gott lo- ben] vnd danck- bar sein. Vnd sin- gen Al-
- ben, [Gott lo- ben] vnd danck- bar sein. Vnd sin- gen Al-
[Gott lo- -ben] vnd danck- bar sein.

35
- le- lu- ja, vnd sin- gen, [Vnd sin- - gen] Al- le- lu-
- le- lu- ja, [Vnd sin- gen Al- - le- lu- ja,] Al-
- le- lu- ja, [Vnd sin- gen Al- - le- lu- ja,] Al-
- le- lu- ja, [Vnd sin- gen Al- - le- lu- ja,]
Vnd sin- gen Al- - le- lu- ja,

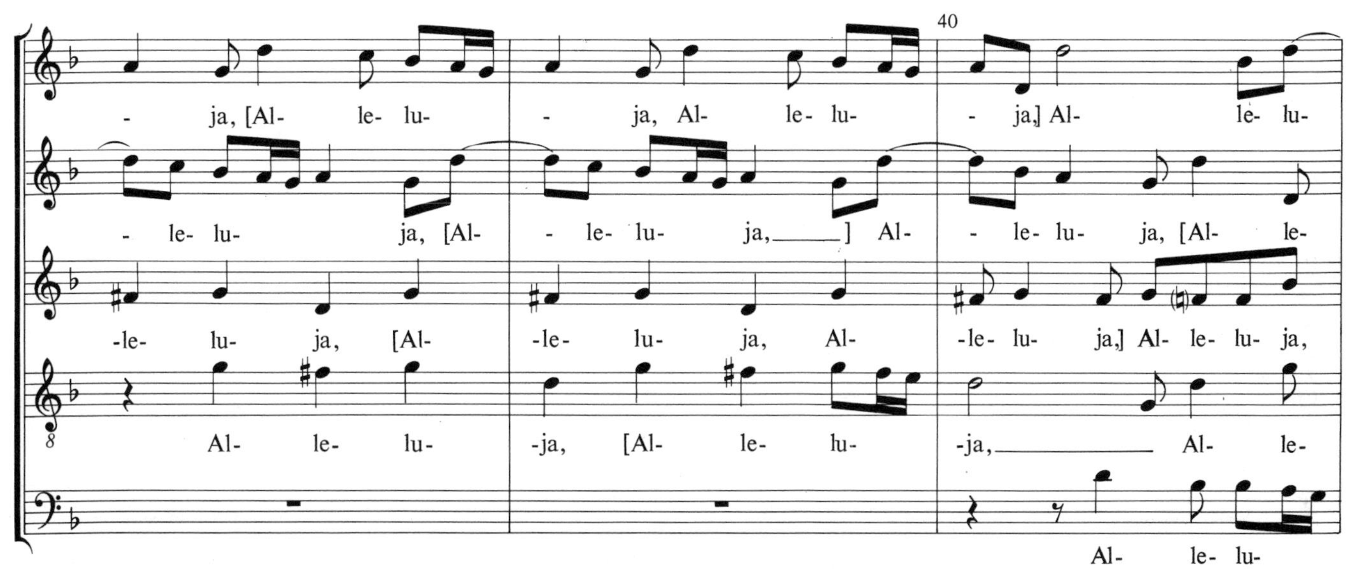
40
- ja, [Al- le- lu- - ja, Al- le- lu- - ja,] Al- le- lu-
- le- lu- ja, [Al- - le- lu- ja,] Al- - le- lu- ja, [Al- le-
-le- lu- ja, [Al- -le- lu- ja, Al- -le- lu- ja,] Al- le- lu- ja,
Al- le- lu- -ja, [Al- le- lu- -ja, Al- le-
Al- le- lu-

[17] In Gottes namen faren wir

Huldrich Braetel
(1495–1544)

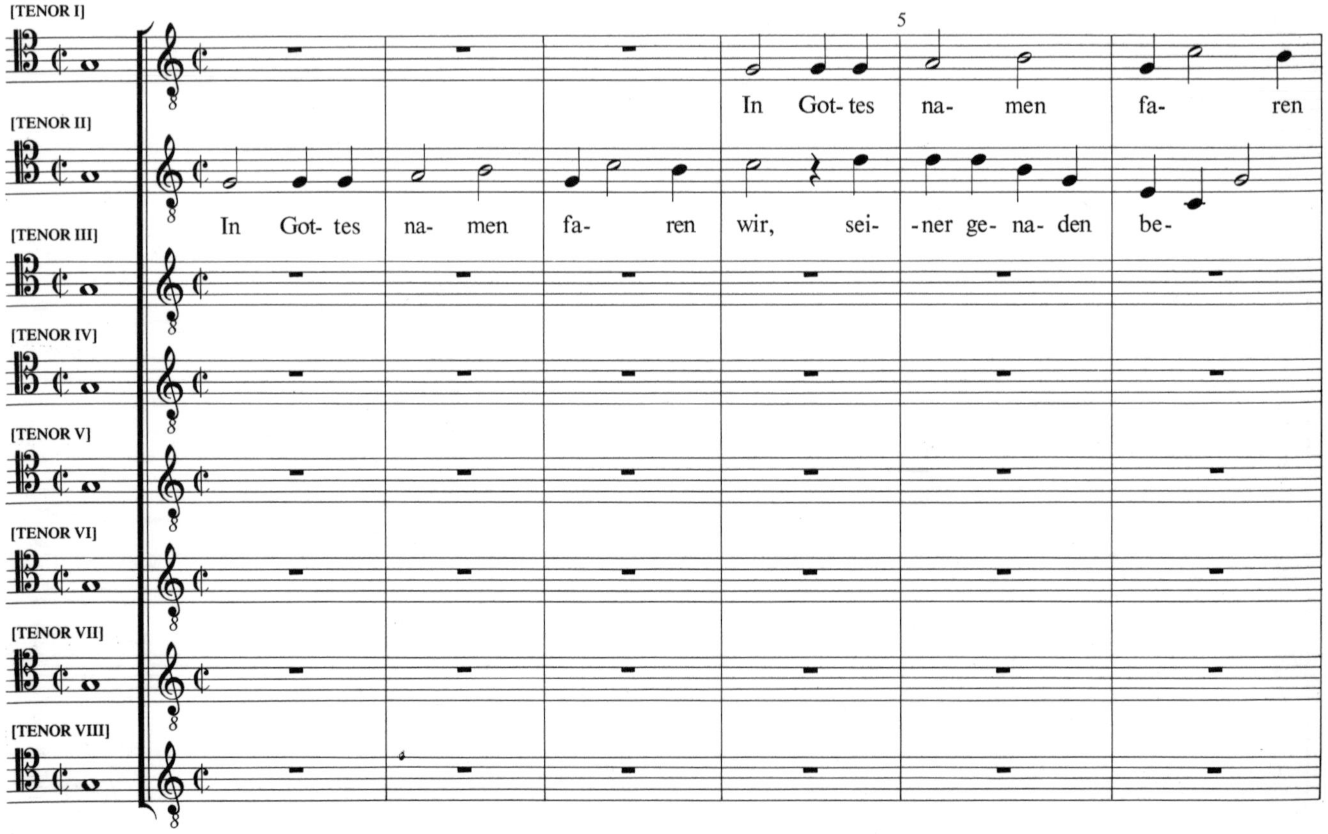

[TENOR I]

5

In Got- tes na- men fa- ren

[TENOR II]

In Got- tes na- men fa- ren wir, sei- -ner ge- na- den be-

[TENOR III]

[TENOR IV]

[TENOR V]

[TENOR VI]

[TENOR VII]

[TENOR VIII]

wir, [sei- -ner ge- na- den be- - ge- -ren wir,
- ge- -ren wir, Das helff vns die___ got- tes- krafft___
In Got- tes na- men fa- ren wir, [sei- -ner ge- na- den
In Got- tes na- men

Das helff vns die___ got- tes- krafft___ vnd das hey-
___ vnd das hey- -li- ge grab, da Gott lag,___
be- - ge- -ren wir, Das helff vns die___
fa- ren wir, [sei- -ner ge- na- den be- - ge-
In Got- tes na- men fa- ren wir, sei-
In Got- tes

20
-li- ge grab, da Gott lag, Ky- ri- -e- lei-
Ky- ri- -e- lei- -son, Chris- te e-
got- tes- krafft vnd das hey- -li- ge grab, da
-ren wir, Das helff vns die got- tes- krafft vnd
-ner ge- na- den be- - ge- -ren wir, Das helff
na- men fa- ren wir, [sei- -ner ge- na- den be-
In Got- tes na- men fa- ren

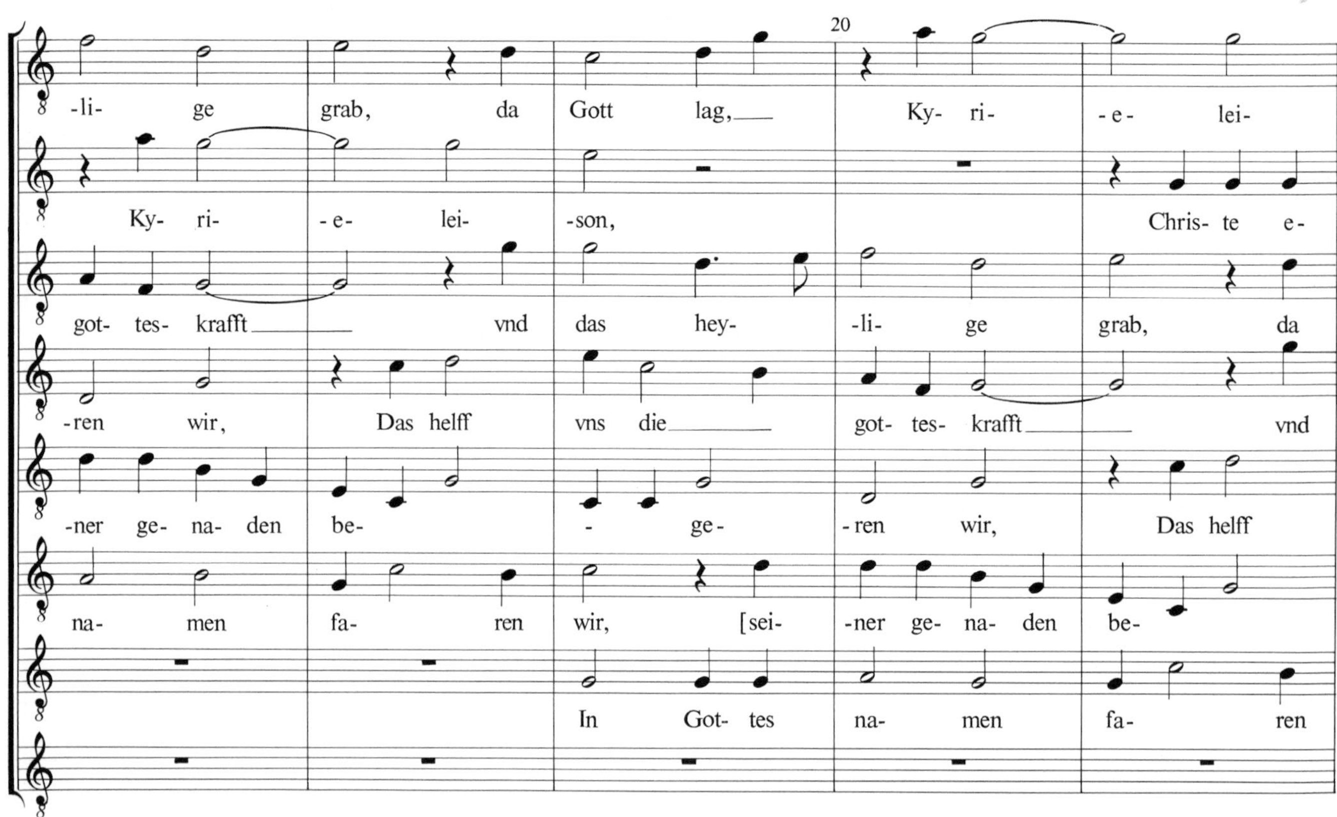

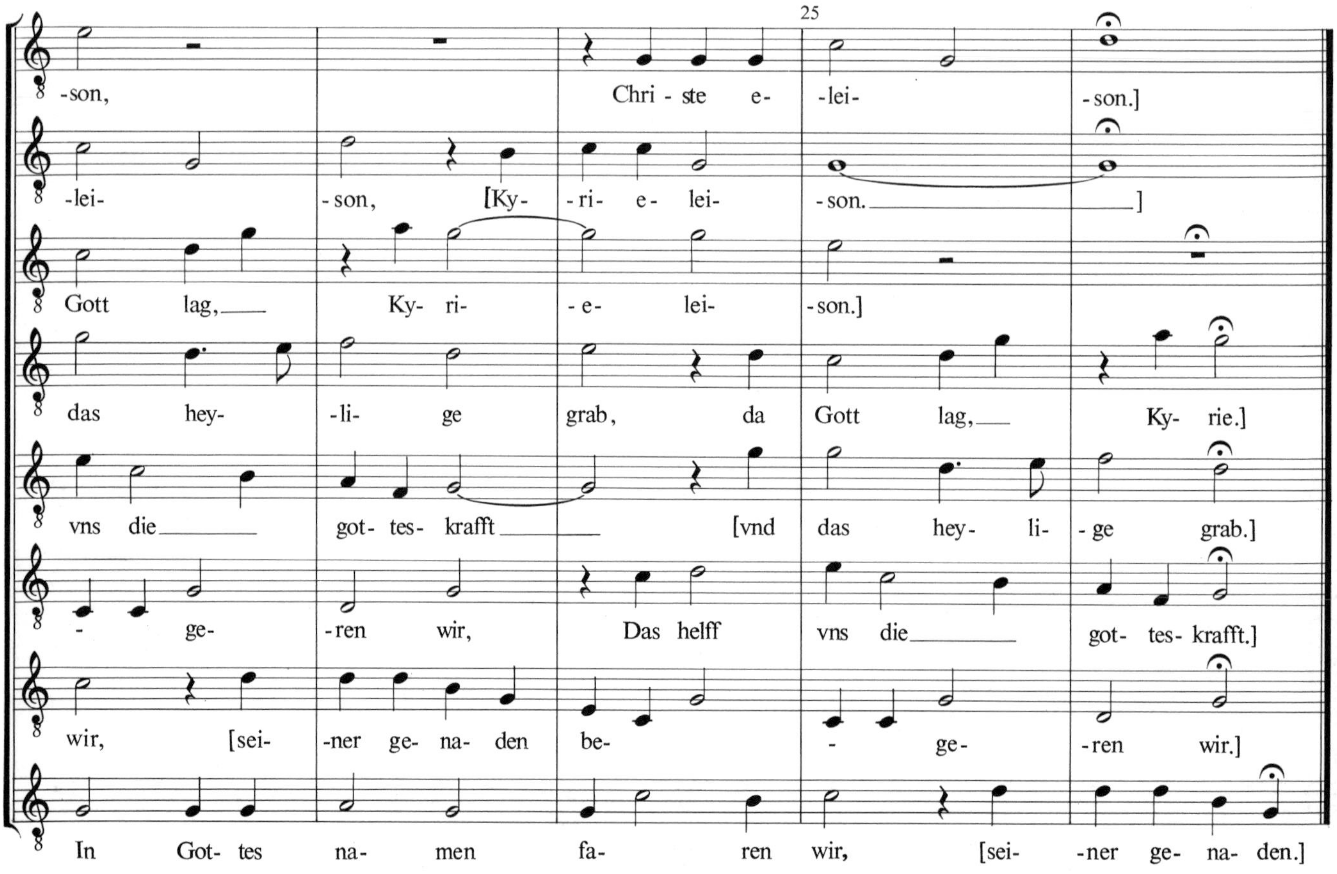

25
-son, Chri - ste e- -lei- -son.]
-lei- -son, [Ky- -ri- e- lei- -son.]
Gott lag, Ky- ri- -e- lei- -son.]
das hey- -li- ge grab, da Gott lag, Ky- rie.]
vns die got- tes- krafft [vnd das hey- li- -ge grab.]
- ge- -ren wir, Das helff vns die got- tes- krafft.]
wir, [sei- -ner ge- na- den be- - ge- -ren wir.]
In Got- tes na- men fa- ren wir, [sei- -ner ge- na- den.]

[18] Missa IV: Christ ist erstanden

Jacob Regnart
(1540–1599)

[Ky- ri- e e- lei- son, Ky- -ri- e- lei- -son,] Ky- ri- e
-son, Ky- ri- e- -lei- -
- son,] Ky- rie e- -lei- son, [e- lei- son,]
-son,] Ky- ri- e e- lei- - son, [Ky- - ri- e- lei-
-e e- lei- son, [Ky- ri- e] e- lei- -son,

15
e- - lei- -son. Chri - ste e- - lei-
-son,] Ky- ri- e e- lei- -son.
Ky- ri- e e- lei- -son.
-son,] Ky- ri- -e e- -lei- son. Chri - ste e-
[Ky- ri- e lei- -son.]

20
- son, [Chri - ste, Chri - -ste e- lei- -son,] Chri - ste e-
Chri - ste e- - lei- son, [Chri - -ste e- lei- - son,] Chri - ste
Chri - -ste e- - -lei- son,
- lei- son, Chri - ste e- - lei- son, [Chri - ste e- lei-
Chri - -ste e- -lei-

25
- -lei- son, [Chri-ste e- lei- son, Chri - - ste e- lei-
e- lei- -son, [e- lei- - son,
[Chri - - ste e- -lei- son, Chri - ste
-son,] Chri - ste e- lei-
- - - son, Chri - ste e -

30
-son, Chri - ste e- lei- son, Chri - ste e- -lei- son, Chri -
Chri - ste e- lei- son, Chri - ste e- lei- son, Chri -
e- - lei- -son,] e- lei- son, [Chri - ste
-son, [Chri-ste e- -lei- son, Chri- -ste e- lei- -son,]
-lei- son, [Chri - - ste e- lei- -son, Chri - ste e- -lei- son,]

35
- ste e- - -lei- son,] Chri - ste e-
-ste e- lei- - son,] Chri - -ste e-
e- - lei- son,] Chri - ste e-
Ky- ri- e e- - lei- son, [Chri- ste e-
Chri - ste e- -

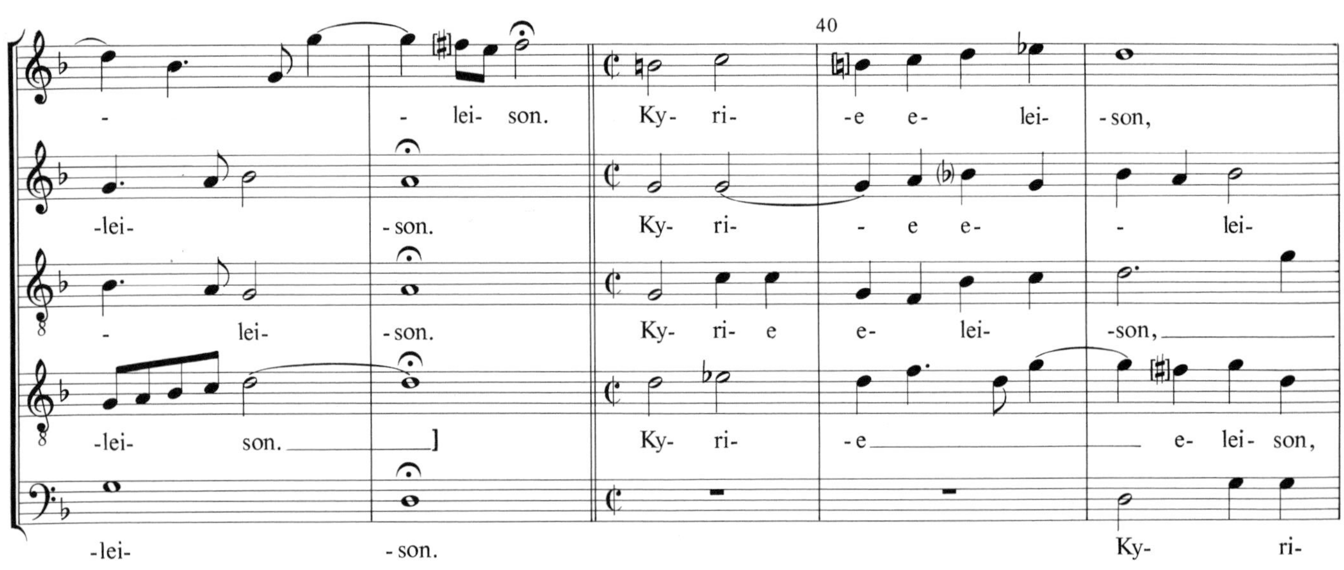
40
- - lei- son. Ky- ri- -e e- lei- -son,
-lei- -son. Ky- ri- - e e- - lei-
- lei- -son. Ky- ri- e e- lei- -son,
-lei- son.] Ky- ri- -e e- lei- son,
-lei- -son. Ky- ri-

45
[Ky- ri- -e e- lei- -son, Ky- ri-
-son, [Ky- ri- -e e- lei- -son, Ky- ri- - e] e-
e- lei- - son,
[Ky- ri- e e- -lei- son,] Ky- ri- -e- lei- son, [Ky- ri- - e e- lei-
-e e- lei- -son, [Ky- -ri- e e- lei- - son,]

50
- e e- - lei- -son, Ky- ri- e e- lei- -son, Ky-
- lei- son, [Ky- - ri- e e- lei- son,]
[Ky- ri- e e- lei- -son,] Ky- ri- e e- -lei- son, [Ky-
- son,]e- - lei- -son, [Ky- - ri- e e- -lei- son,]
Ky- ri- e e- - lei- son, [Ky- ri- -e- lei-

-ri- e e- lei- -son,] Ky- -ri- e e- -lei- son, [Ky-
e- lei- son, [Ky- ri- -e e- lei- - son,]
-ri- e e- - - lei- son,] Ky- ri- e
Ky- ri- -e e- lei- - son,
-son, Ky- ri- - e e- lei- - son,

55
- ri- e e- - - lei- - son,] Ky-
Ky- ri- e e- lei- son, [Ky- ri- - e e- lei-
e- lei- -son, [Ky- ri- -e e- - lei- son,]
[Ky- -ri- e - lei- -son, Ky-
Ky- -ri- e- lei- -son,] Ky- - ri- e e-

60
-ri- e e- - lei- son, [Ky- -ri- e e- - lei- -son.]
- son, Ky- -rie e- lei- -son.]
Ky- ri- e e- lei- -son, [Ky- -ri-] e- lei- -son.
-ri- e- - lei- son,] Ky- ri- -e e- lei- -son.
-lei- - - - -son.

Gloria

bo- nae
bo- - nae vo- lun-
Et in ter- ra pax ho- mi- ni- -bus bo- nae vo- lun-
Et in ter- ra pax ho- mi- ni- -bus
Et in ter- ra pax ho- - mi- ni- -bus bo-

5
vo- lun- ta- - tis, [bo- nae vo- - lun- ta- -tis.] Lau- da- mus
- ta- tis, [bo- -nae vo- lun- - - ta- tis.]
-ta- tis, [bo- -nae vo- lun- - ta- tis.] Lau- da-
bo- nae vo- lun- -ta- -tis. Lau-
-nae vo- lun- ta- - - tis. Lau-

10
te, [lau-da- mus te.] Be- ne- di- ci- mus te. A- do- -ra- mus te. Glo-
Lau- da- mus te. Be- ne- di- ci- mus te. A- do- -ra- mus te. Glo- ri-
-mus te. Be- ne- di- -ci- mus te.
-da- mus te. Be- -ne- di- ci- mus te. A- do- -ra- mus te. Glo-
-da- mus te. Be- -ne- di- ci- mus te.

-ri- fi- ca- mus te. Gra- ti- as a- gi- mus ti- bi pro- -pter ma- gnam,
-fi- ca- mus te. Gra- ti- as a- gi- mus ti- bi pro-
Gra- ti- -as a- gi- mus ti- bi pro-
-ri- fi- ca- mus te. pro-
Gra- ti- as a- gi- mus ti- bi pro-

[pro- pter ma- -gnam] glo- ri- am tu- am. Do- mi- -ne De- us, Rex
-pter ma- gnam glo- ri- am tu- am. Do- mi- -ne De- us,
-pter ma- -gnam glo- ri- am tu- am.
-pter ma- gnam glo- riam tu- -am. Do- mi- -ne De- us, Rex
-pter ma- gnam glo- -ri- am tu- am. Do- mi- ne De- us, Rex

cae- -le- stis, De- -us Pa- ter
Rex cae- -le- stis, De- us Pa- - ter o-
Rex cae- le- -stis, De- - us Pa- ter
cae- le- - stis, Rex cae- le- -stis, De-us
cae- - le- stis, De- us Pa- -ter o- mni- po-

o- mni-po-tens. Do- mi- ne Fi- li, [Do- mi-ne
- mni- po- -tens. Do- mi- ne, Do- mi- -ne Fi- li u-
o- mni- po- -tens. Do- - mi- ne Fi- li u- ni- ge- ni- te
Pa- ter o- mni- po- -tens. Do- mi- ne Fi- -li u-
-tens. Do- mi- ne Fi- li u- ni- -ge- ni- te

30
Fi- li] u- -ni- ge- ni- te Je- -
-ni- ge- ni- - te Je- su Chri- ste,
Je- - su Chri- ste, [Je- su
-ni- ge- ni- -te, [u- ni- ge- ni- te] Je- su Chri-
Je- - su Chri-

35
-su Chri- - ste. Do- mi- ne De- -us, A- gnus
[Je- su Chri- - ste.] Do- - mi- ne De- us, A- gnus, A-
Chri- - ste.] Do-mi- ne De- us, A- gnus De- i,
- - ste. Do- - mi- ne De- us,
- ste. Do- mi- ne De- -us, A- gnus De- - i, A- gnus

40
De- i, Fi- - li- us Pa- -tris, Fi-
-gnus De- -i, Fi- lius
Fi- li- us Pa- tris, [Fi- lius Pa- tris,] Fi- - li- us
A- gnus De- i, Fi- lius Pa- - -tris, [Fi- lius
De- i, Fi- -lius Pa- - tris,

45
- li- us Pa- tris, [Fi- li- us Pa- -tris.]
Pa- - -tris, [Fi- lius Pa- - -tris.]
Pa- tris, Fi- - li- us Pa- -tris.
Pa- tris,] Fi- lius Pa- - - tris.
Fi- - lius Pa- - tris.

50
Qui tol- -lis pec- ca- ta mun- di, mi- - se- re- re, mi- se- re-
Qui tol- lis pec- ca- ta mun- -di, mi- - se- re- re,
mi-
Qui tol- lis pec- ca- -ta mun- di, mi- se- -re- re no-
Qui tol- lis pec- ca- -ta mun- di, mi- se- -re- re no-

55
-re,___ [mi- se- re- re no- bis,] no- -bis. Qui tol- lis pec- ca- -ta mun- di,
mi- se- re- re no- bis. Qui tol- -lis pec- ca- ta, qui tol- lis pec-
- se- re- re no- bis. Qui tol- lis, qui tol- -lis pec- ca- ta mun-
- bis. Qui tol- lis sus-
- bis. Qui tol- lis pec- ca- -ta mun- di,

sus- - ci- pe de- pre- ca- ti- o- - nem no-
-ca- ta mun- -di, sus- ci- -pe de- pre- ca- -tio- nem no-
-di, sus- ci- -pe de- pre- -ca -ti- o- nem no- stram._
- ci- pe de- pre- -ca- ti- o- nem no- stram.___
sus- ci- -pe de- pre- -ca- ti- o- nem no-

60
-stram. Qui se- des ad dex- te- -ram Pa- tris, mi- - se- re- re
-stram. Qui se- des ad dex- te- ram Pa- -tris, mi- se- re- re no- bis, [mi- se-
___ Qui se- des ad dex- te- ram Pa- -tris, mi- se- re- re, mi- se- re-
___ mi- se- re- -re no- bis, [mi- se-
-stram. mi- se- -re- re

65
no- - bis. Quo- ni- am tu so- lus, so- lus
-re- re no- -bis.] Quo-ni- am tu so- -lus san- ctus,
-re no- bis. Quo-ni- am tu so- -lus san- ctus, [tu so- lus san- ctus, tu so- lus
-re- re no- bis.] Quo-ni- am tu so-
no- -bis. Quo-ni- -am tu so- lus san- -ctus.

70
san- ctus. Tu so- lus Do-mi- nus. Tu so- -lus al- -tis -si -mus,
[tu so- lus san- ctus.] Tu so- lus Do-mi- nus. Tu so- lus al- tis- si- -mus, al- tis-
san- ctus.] Tu so- lus Do- mi- nus. Tu so- -lus al- tis- si-
-lus san- ctus. Tu so- lus Do- mi- nus, [tu so- lus Do- -mi- nus.] Tu so-
Tu so- lus Do- mi- -nus. Tu so- lus al- tis- - si- mus,

75
Je- su Chri- ste, [Je- su Chri- ste.] Cum San- cto Spi- ri-
-si- mus, Je- su Chri- - ste, Je- -su Chri- ste. Cum San- cto, cum San-
-mus, Je- - su Chri- -ste. Cum San- cto Spi- ri-
-lus al- tis- - si- mus Je- - su Chri- - ste.
Je- - su Chri- - ste.

80
-tu, in glo-ri- -a, [in glo-ri- -a] De- i Pa- -tris, [in glo-ri-
-cto Spi- ri- tu, Spi- ri- tu in glo- ri- a De- -i Pa- tris. A- men.
-tu, cum San-cto Spi- ri- tu in glo-ri- a De- i Pa- tris. A- men.
Cum San- cto Spi- ri- tu in glo-ri- a De- i Pa- tris. A-
Cum San- cto Spi- ri- tu, in glo- ri- a, in

85
-a De- i Pa- - tris. A- - - men, A-
[in glo-ri- a De- i Pa- tris,] in glo- - ri- a De- -i Pa-
[in glo-ri- a De- -i Pa- tris] A- - men, A- -
-men, Pa- tris. A- - -men, A- - men, A-
glo-ri- a De- i Pa- -tris. A-

90
- -men, A- -
-tris, [in glo- ri- a De- i Pa- -tris.] A- men,
- -men, A- - men, A-
- - - men, A-
- men, [A- - men, A- -

95
-men, A- - men,] A- -men, A- - men.
De- - i Pa- - tris. A- -men.
-men, A- - -men.
- - -men, A- - men, A- men.
- - men,] A- - -men.

Credo

5
fa- -cto- rem cae- li et ter- rae,
fa- cto- rem cae- li et ter- rae, [fa-
Pa- -trem o- mni- po- -ten- tem, fa- cto- rem, fa- - cto- rem cae- li et
fa-
Pa- trem o- -mni- po- -ten- tem, fa- -cto- rem cae- -li et ter-

[fa- cto- rem cae- li et ter- -rae,]
-cto- rem cae- -li,] cae- li et ter- rae, vi- si- bi- li- um,
ter- rae, et ter- - rae, vi- si-
- cto- rem cae- -li et ter- -rae, vi- si- -bi- li- um
-rae, vi- -si- bi- li- um, o-

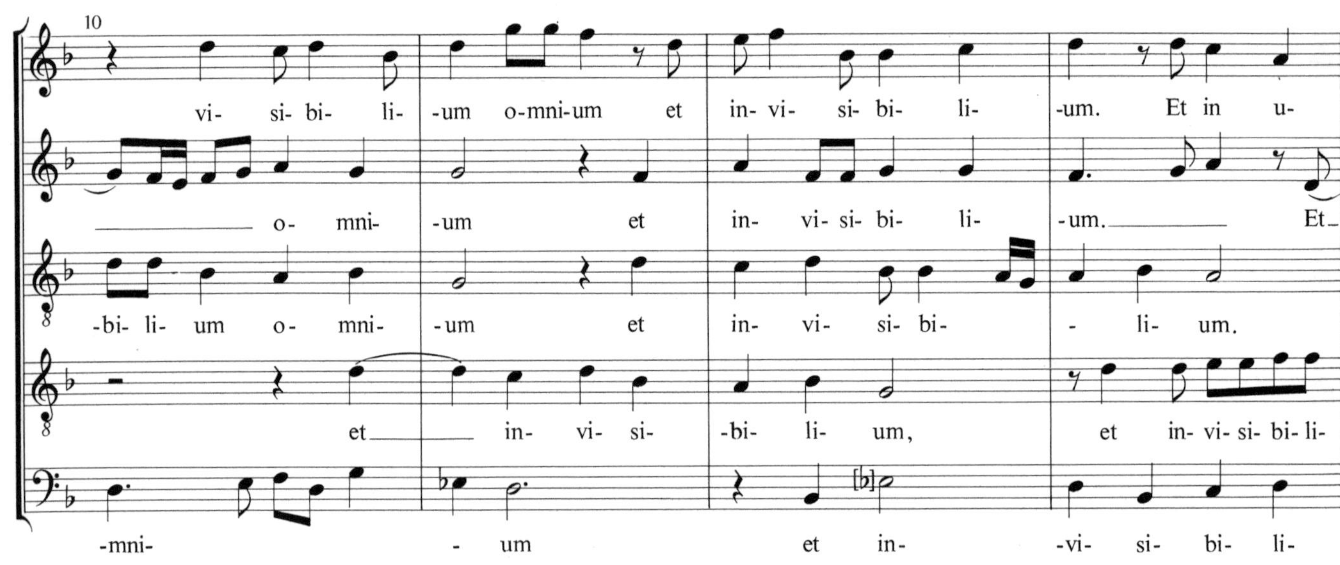
10
vi- si- bi- li- -um o-mni-um et in- vi- si- bi- li- -um. Et in u-
o- mni- -um et in- vi- si- bi- li- -um. Et
-bi- li- um o- mni- -um et in- vi- si- bi- - li- um.
et in- vi- si- -bi- li- um, et in- vi- si- bi- li-
-mni- - um et in- -vi- si- bi- li-

15
-num Do- mi- -num Je- sum Chri- stum, Je- - sum Chri- - stum, Fi- lium,
in u- num Do- - mi- num Je- sum Chri- -
Et in u- num Do- mi- -num Je- - sum Chri- -stum, Fi- li-
-um. Je- - sum Chri- -
-um. Je- sum Chri- - stum,

20
Fi- li- um De- -i u- ni- -ge- ni- tum. Et
-stum. Fi- li- -um De- i u- ni- -ge- ni- tum, u- ni- -ge- ni- tum.
-um De- i u- ni- -ge- ni- tum, [Fili- um De- i u- ni- -ge- ni- tum.] Et
-stum. Fi- - li- um De- i u- ni- ge- ni- tum, [u- - ni- ge- ni- tum.]
Fi- li- um De- -i u- ni- ge- ni- tum, u- ni- -ge- ni- tum.

25
— ex Pa-tre na- -tum, na- tum an- -te o- mni- -a,
Et ex Pa- tre na- tum an- te o- mni- a sae- - cu- la. De- um
ex Pa- tre na- tum an- -te o- mni- a sae- cu- la.___
Et ex Pa- tre na- tum De- -um de De-
Et ex Pa- tre na- tum an- -te o- mni- a sae- cu- la. De-

30
o- mni- a sae- cu- la, lu- men de lu- mi- ne, De- - um de De-
de De- o, lu- men de___ lu- mi- ne, De- um ve- rum de De- o
lu- men de lu- mi- ne, De- -um ve- rum de De- o ve- ro.
-o, lu- men de lu-mi- ne, De- um ve- -rum de___ De-
-um de De- -o, lu- men de lu- mi- ne, De- um ve- -rum de De- o

35
- o ve- ro. Ge- ni-tum, non fa- ctum, con- sub- - stan- ti- a-
ve- ro. Ge- -ni- tum, non___ fa- ctum, con- sub- -stan- tia- lem Pa-
Ge- - ni- tum, non fa- ctum,
-o ve- ro. Ge- ni- tum, non fa- ctum, con- - sub- stan- ti- -a- lem
ve- ro.

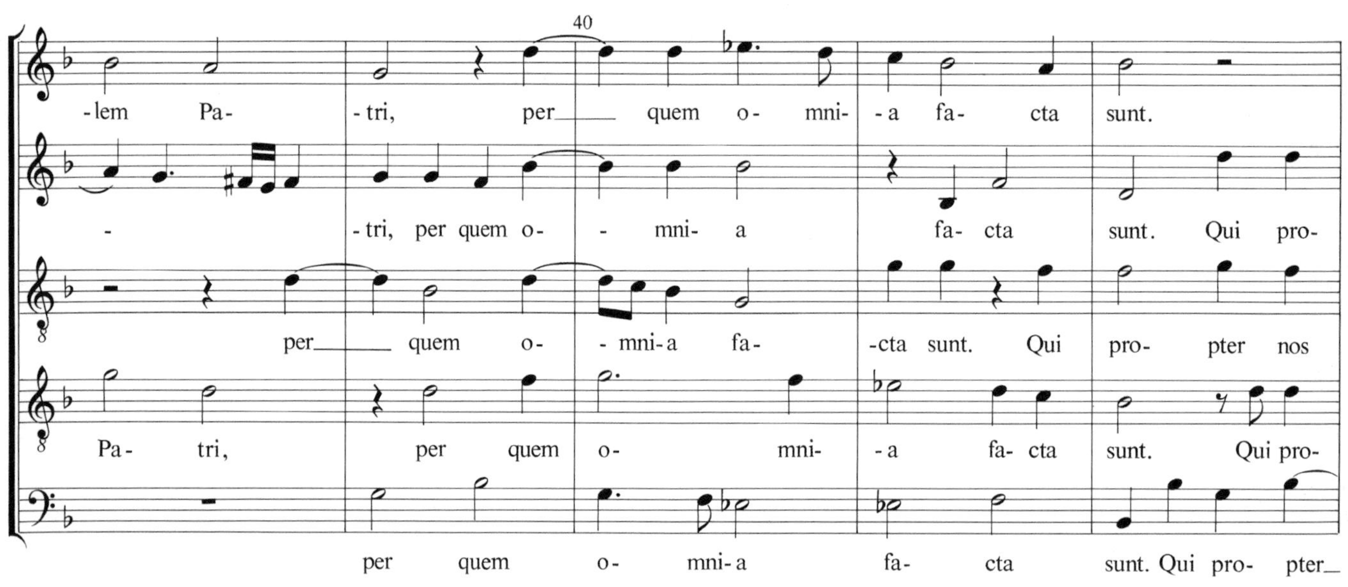
40
-lem Pa- -tri, per quem o- mni- -a fa- cta sunt.
- -tri, per quem o- - mni- a fa- cta sunt. Qui proper quem o- - mni-a fa- -cta sunt. Qui pro- pter nos
Pa- tri, per quem o- mni- -a fa- cta sunt. Qui proper quem o- mni- a fa- cta sunt. Qui pro- pter

45
Qui pro- pter no- stram sa- lu- tem de- scen-
-pter nos ho- mi- -nes, et pro- pter no-stram sa- lu- -tem de- scen-dit de cae- lis,
ho- mi- -nes, et pro-pter no- stram sa- lu- -tem de- - scen- dit de
-pter nos ho- mi- -nes, de- scen- -
nos ho- mi- nes, de- -scen- dit de cae-

50
- dit, [de- - scen- -dit] de cae- -
[de- scen- dit de cae- lis, de- scen- dit de cae- lis,] de- scen-
cae- lis, [de- scen- dit de cae- lis,
[- dit, de- scen- dit] de cae- -lis, [de cae-
-lis, [de- -scen- dit de cae- lis, de- scen- dit

25
— ex Pa-tre na- -tum, na- tum an- -te o- mni- -a,
Et ex Pa- tre na- tum an- te o- mni-a sae- - cu- la. De- um
ex Pa- tre na- tum an- -te o- mni- a sae- cu- la.
Et ex Pa- tre na- tum De- -um de De-
Et ex Pa- tre na- tum an- -te o- mni- a sae- cu- la. De-

30
o- mni- a sae- cu- la. lu- men de lu- mi- ne, De- - um de De-
de De- o, lu- men de lu- mi- ne, De- um ve- rum de De-o
lu- men de lu- mi- ne, De- -um ve- rum de De- o ve- ro.
-o, lu- men de lu-mi- ne, De- um ve- -rum de De-
-um de De- -o, lu- men de lu- mi- ne, De- um ve- -rum de De- o

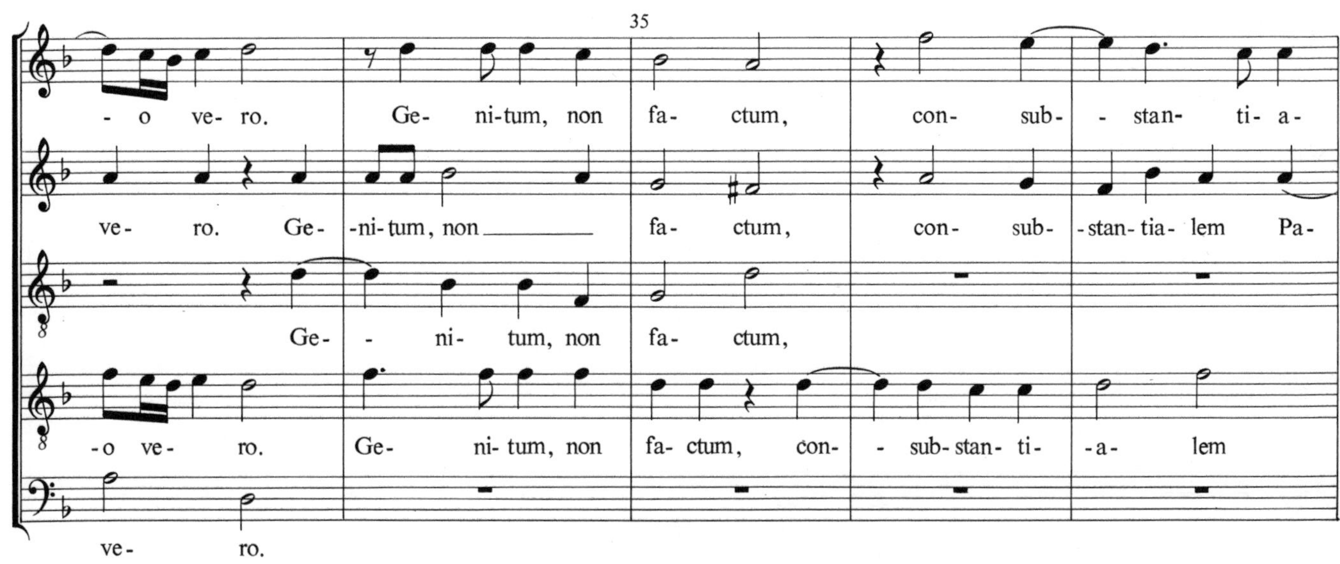
35
- o ve- ro. Ge- ni-tum, non fa- ctum, con- sub- - stan- ti- a-
ve- ro. Ge- -ni- tum, non fa- ctum, con- sub- -stan- tia- lem Pa-
Ge- - ni- tum, non fa- ctum,
-o ve- ro. Ge- ni- tum, non fa- ctum, con- - sub- stan- ti- -a- lem
ve- ro.

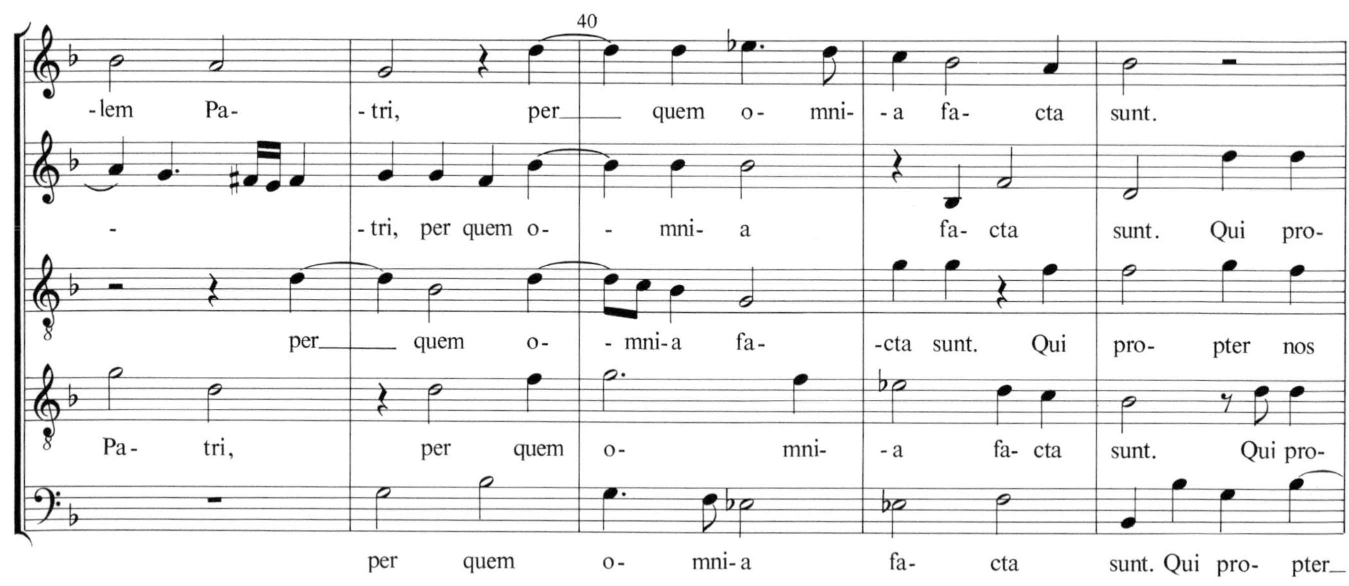
40
-lem Pa- -tri, per quem o- mni- -a fa- cta sunt.
- -tri, per quem o- - mni- a fa- cta sunt. Qui proper quem o- - mni-a fa- -cta sunt. Qui pro- pter nos
Pa- tri, per quem o- mni- -a fa- cta sunt. Qui proper quem o- mni-a fa- cta sunt. Qui pro- pter

45
Qui pro- pter no- stram sa- lu- tem de- scen-
-pter nos ho- mi- -nes, et pro- pter no- stram sa- lu- -tem de- scen-dit de cae- lis,
ho- mi- -nes, et pro-pter no- stram sa- lu- -tem de- - scen- dit de
-pter nos ho- mi- -nes, de- scen- -
nos ho- mi- nes, de- -scen- dit de cae-

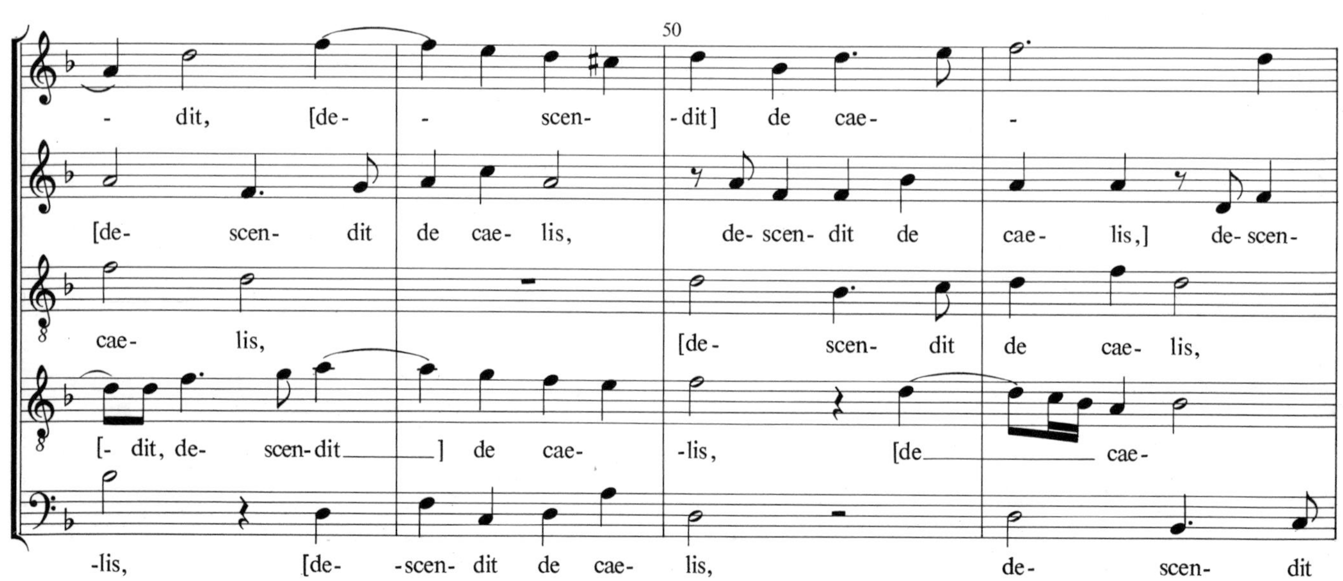
50
- dit, [de- - scen- -dit] de cae- -
[de- scen- dit de cae- lis, de- scen- dit de cae- lis,] de- scen-
cae- lis, [de- scen- dit de cae- lis,
[- dit, de- scen-dit] de cae- -lis, [de cae-
-lis, [de- -scen- dit de cae- lis, de- scen- dit

55
-lis, [de cae- - - lis,] de cae- -lis.
-dit de cae- lis, [de- scen- dit de cae- -lis.] Et in- car-
de-scen-dit de cae- -lis,] de- - scen- dit de cae- lis.
-lis,] de- -scen- dit de cae- -lis, [de cae- -lis.] Et
de cae- lis, de- scen- dit de cae- -lis.] Et in- car-

60
Et in- car- na- tus est de Spi- ri- -tu San-
-na- tus est de Spi- ri- -tu San- -cto, de Spi-
de Spi- ri- tu San- cto
in- car- -na- tus est de Spi-ri- tu San- -cto ex
-na- tus est de Spi- ri- -tu San- cto

65
-cto ex Ma- ri- - a Vir- gi- -ne: Et ho-
-ri- tu San- cto ex Ma- ri- a Vir- gi- -ne: Et ho- mo
ex Ma- ri- a, ex Ma- ri- - a Vir- gi- -ne: Et ho-
Ma- ri- - a Vir- gi- -ne: Et ho-mo fa- ctus
ex Ma- ri- -a Vir- - gi- ne:

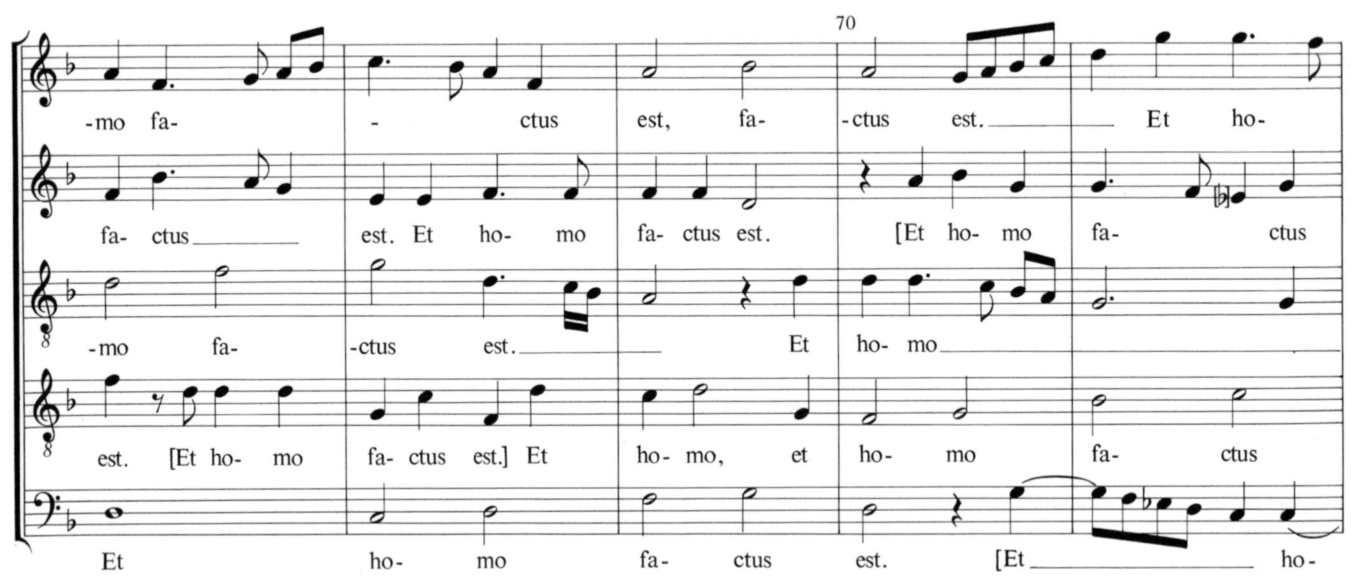
70
-mo fa- - ctus est, fa- -ctus est. Et ho-
fa- ctus est. Et ho- mo fa- ctus est. [Et ho- mo fa- ctus
-mo fa- -ctus est. Et ho- mo
est. [Et ho- mo fa- ctus est.] Et ho- mo, et ho- mo fa- ctus
Et ho- mo fa- ctus est. [Et ho-

75
- mo fa- ctus est. Cru- ci- fi- - xus e- ti- -am pro
est.] Cru- ci- fi- - xus e- ti- -am, e- ti- am
fa- ctus est.
est. Cru- ci- fi- - xus e- ti-
- mo fa- ctus est.]

80
no- -bis, sub Pon- ti- -o Pi- la- -to:
pro no- bis, sub Pon- ti- -o Pi- -la- to: pas- sus,
sub Pon- ti- o Pi- -la- -to: pas- sus,
-am pro no- bis, sub Pon- - ti- o Pi- - la- -to: pas-

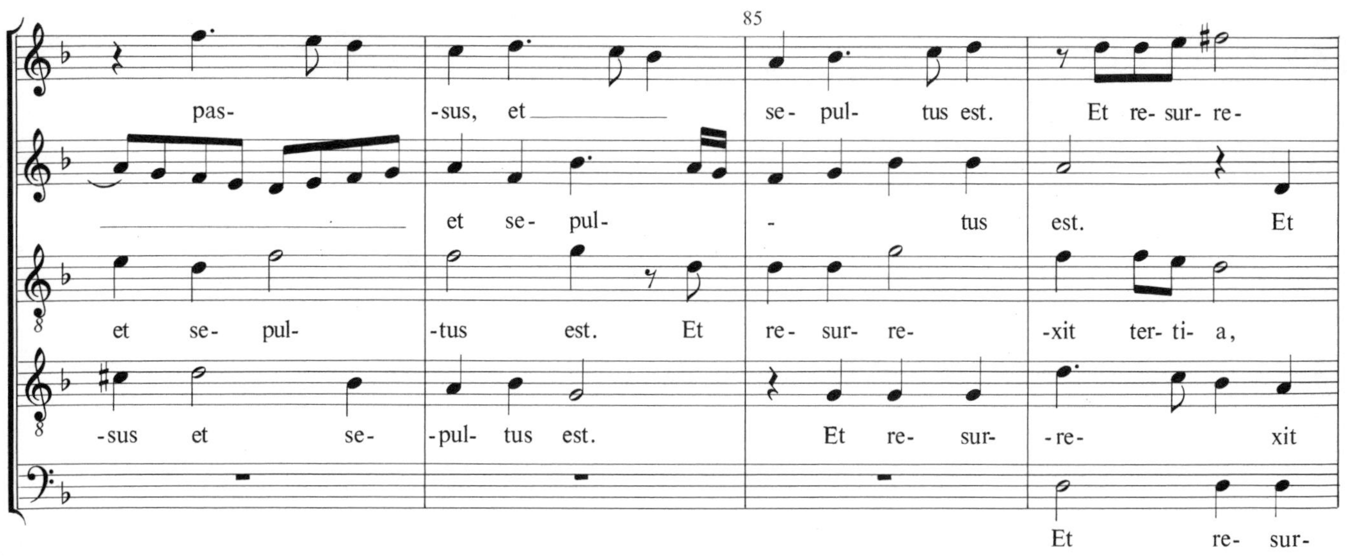
85
pas- -sus, et se- pul- tus est. Et re- sur- re-
et se- pul- - tus est. Et
et se- pul- -tus est. Et re- sur- re- -xit ter- ti- a,
-sus et se- -pul- tus est. Et re- sur- -re- xit
Et re- sur-

90
-xit ter- -ti- a di- - e, se- cun- dum,
re- sur- re- xit ter- ti- a di- e, ter- ti-
et re- sur- re- - xit ter- - ti- a die, se- cun- dum Scri-
ter- tia di- -e, se- cun- dum
-re- xit ter- ti- -a di- e, se- cun- dum

95
se- cun- dum Scri- ptu- ras. Et a- scen- - dit in
- a di- e, se- cun- - dum Scri- ptu- -ras. Et
-ptu- ras, se- cun- -dum Scri- -ptu- ras. Et a- scen- dit
Scri- ptu- ras, se- - cun- dum Scri- ptu- ras, Scri- ptu- -ras.
Scri- ptu- - ras, [se- -cun- dum Scri- ptu- ras.] Et a- scen-

100
caе- -lum, [et a- scen- -dit in cae- lum:] se-
a- scen-dit in cae- lum, [et a- scen- - dit in cae- -lum:] sein cae- - - lum, et a- scen- dit in cae-
Et a- scen- - dit in cae- -lum: se-
- dit in cae- -lum, [et a- scen- dit in cae- - lum:]

105
-det ad dex- te- -ram Pa- -tris, [se- - det ad dex- - te- ram
-det ad dex- te- -ram Pa- -tris, [se- -det ad dex- te- -ram Pa-
-lum: se- -det ad dex- te- -ram Pa- tris, [et se- det ad dex-te- ram
-det ad dex- te- -ram Pa- tris, [et a- scen- -dit in cae- lum:] ad dex- te-
se- -det ad dex- te- -ram Pa-

110
Pa- -tris,] se- det ad dex- te- ram Pa- - -tris.
-tris,] se- - det ad dex- te- ram Pa- -tris.
Pa- tris,] se- -det ad dex- te- -ram Pa- tris.
- ram Pa- -tris, se- -det ad dex- te- -ram Pa- -tris.
-tris, [se- det ad dex- te- ram Pa- -tris.]

115
Et i- te-rum ven- -tu- rus est cum glo- ri- a ju- -di-
Et i- te- -rum ven- tu- rus est cum glo- ri-
Et i- te- -rum ven- tu- rus est cum glo- ri- -a ju- di- ca- -re vi-

120
-ca- re vi- vos et mor- tu- -os: cu- -jus re-
-a ju- di- ca- -re vi- vos et mor- tu- -os: cu- jus re- -gni non e-
- vos et mor- tu- -os: cu- jus re- -gni non e- rit

-gni, cu- jus re- -gni non e- rit fi- nis, [cu-
- rit fi- nis, cu- jus re- gni non
fi- nis, cu- - jus re- - gni, cu-

125
-jus re- - gni non e- rit fi- nis,] cu-
e- rit fi- nis, non e- - rit fi- nis, cu- jus re-
-jus re- gni non e- rit fi- nis, non e- rit fi- -nis, cu- jus re-

130
-jus re- -gni non e- rit fi- -nis.
-gni non e- rit fi- nis, [fi- - - nis.]
-gni non e- rit fi- nis, non e- -rit fi- -nis.

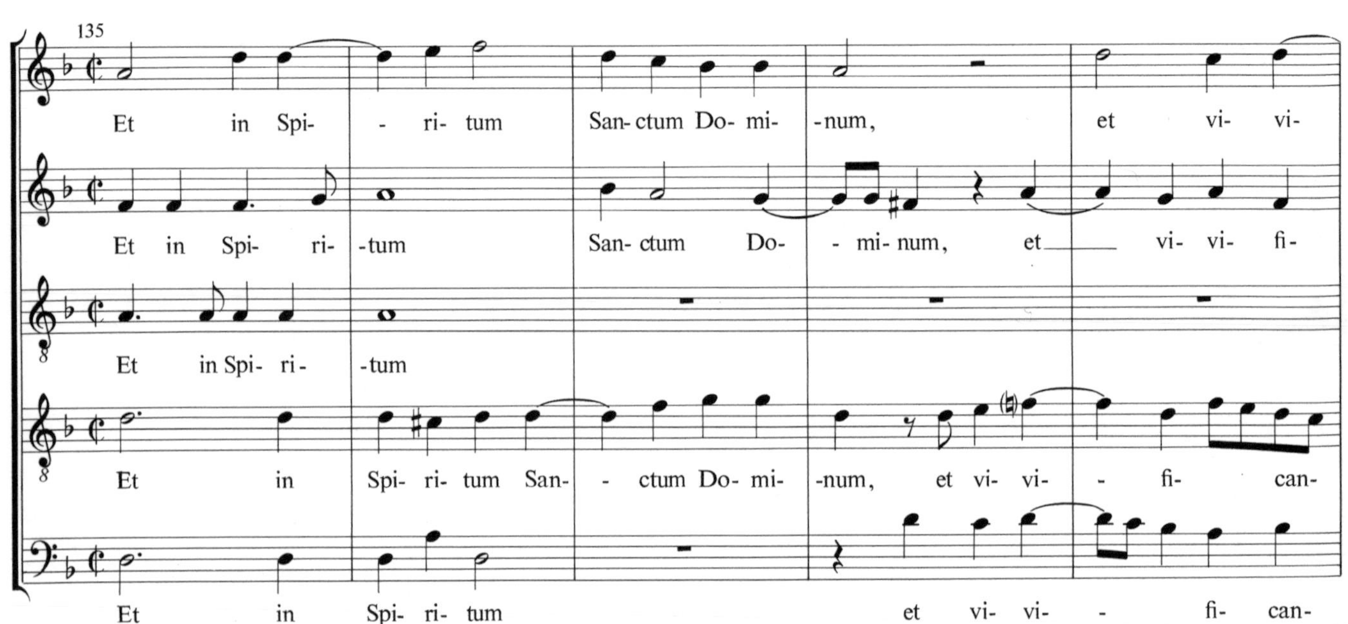
135
Et in Spi- - ri- tum San- ctum Do- mi- -num, et vi- vi-
Et in Spi- ri- -tum San- ctum Do- - mi- num, et vi- vi- fi-
Et in Spi- ri- -tum
Et in Spi- ri- tum San- - ctum Do- mi- -num, et vi- vi- - fi- can-
Et in Spi- ri- tum et vi- vi- - fi- can-

140
- fi- can- tem: qui ex Pa- tre, Fi- li- o- que pro- -
-can- tem, [et vi- vi- fi- -can- tem:] qui ex Pa- tre, qui ex Pa- tre Fi-
et vi- vi- - fi- can- -tem: qui ex Pa- -tre Fi- li- o-
- tem, vi- vi- -fi- can- tem: qui ex Pa- tre Fi- -li- o- que pro- ce- dit.
-tem, et vi- vi- fi- -can- tem: qui ex Pa- tre Fi- li- o- que

145
- ce- -dit. Qui cum Pa- tre, et Fi- li- o si- mul
- li- o que pro- ce- -dit. Qui cum Pa- tre, et Fi- li- o si-
-que pro- ce- -dit. Qui cum Pa- tre,
Qui cum Pa-tre, et Fi- lio si- mul a- do- -ra- tur,
pro- ce- dit. Qui cum Pa- -tre, et Fi- li- o si- mul a- do- ra-

150
a- do- ra- tur, et con- glo- -ri- fi- ca- -tur, qui lo- cu-
- mul a- do- -ra- tur, et con-glo- -ri- fi- ca- tur, qui lo-
et Fi- li- o si- - mul a- do- ra- tur, et con-glo- ri- fi- -ca- tur,
et con- -glo- ri- fi- ca- -tur, qui lo- cu-
-tur, a- do- ra- -tur et con- glo- -ri- fi- ca- -tur, qui

155
-tus est per Pro- phe- - -tas.
-cu- tus est per Pro- -phe- tas. Et u- nam, san-
qui lo- cu- tus est per Pro-phe- -tas.
-tus est per Pro- phe- tas, [per Pro-phe- -tas.] Et u- nam san-
lo- cu- tus est per Pro- phe- -tas. Et u- nam san-

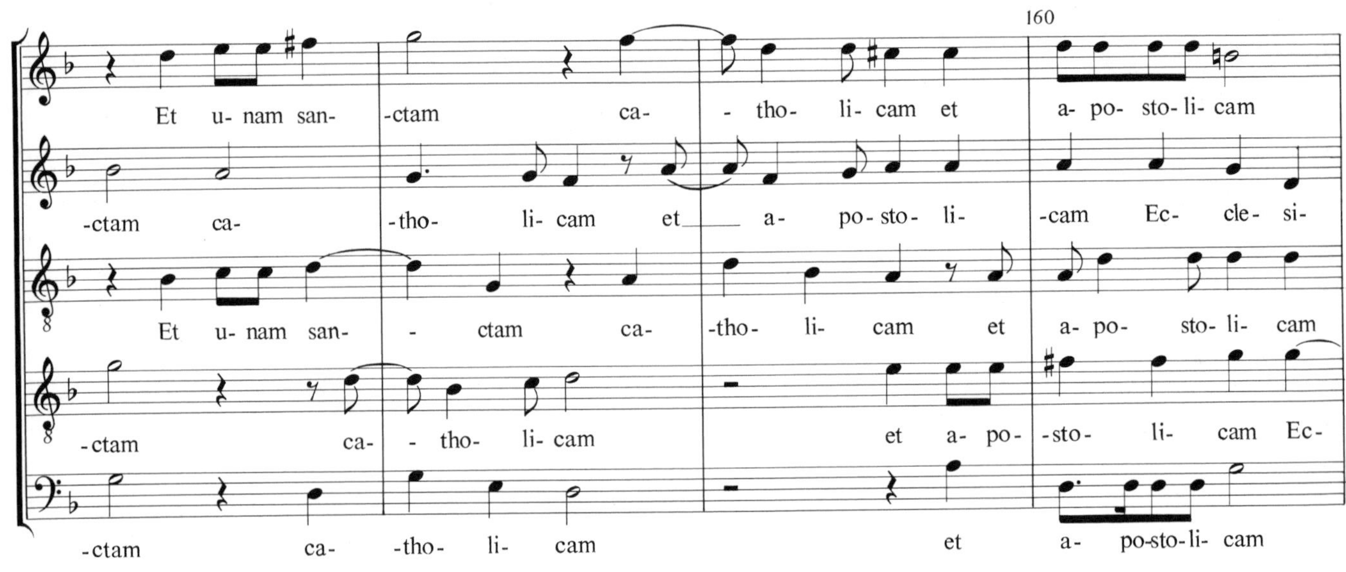
160
Et u- nam san- -ctam ca- - tho- li- cam et a- po- sto- li- cam
-ctam ca- -tho- li- cam et a- po- sto- li- -cam Ec- cle- si-
Et u- nam san- - ctam ca- -tho- li- cam et a- po- sto- li- cam
-ctam ca- - tho- li- cam et a- po- -sto- li- cam Ec-
-ctam ca- -tho- li- cam et a- po-sto- li- cam

165
Ec- cle- si- am. Con- fi- te- -or u- - num ba- - ptis-
-am. Con- fi- - te- or, con- -fi- te- or u- -num ba-
Ec- -cle- si- am. Con- -fi- te- or
- cle- - si- am. Con- fi- te- -or u- num ba- pti-
Ec- cle- si- am. Con- -fi- te- or

170
- ma in re-mis- si- -o- nem pec- ca- -to- rum. Et
- pti- sma in re-mis- si- -o- nem pec-ca-to- -rum. Et
in re-mis- si- -o- - nem pec- ca- to- - rum.
-sma in re-mis-si- o- nem pec- ca- to- rum, pec- ca- -to- rum. Et
in re- -mis- si- o- -nem pec- -ca- to- -rum. Et

ex- spe- -cto re- sur- rec- ti- -o- nem mor-
ex- spe- - cto, re- sur- -re- cti- o- -nem mor- tu-
Et ex- -spe- cto re- sur- -re- cti- o- nem mor- tu- o-
ex- spe- cto re- sur- re- cti- -o- nem mor- - tu- o-
ex- spe- -cto re- sur- -re- cti- o- -nem mor- tu-

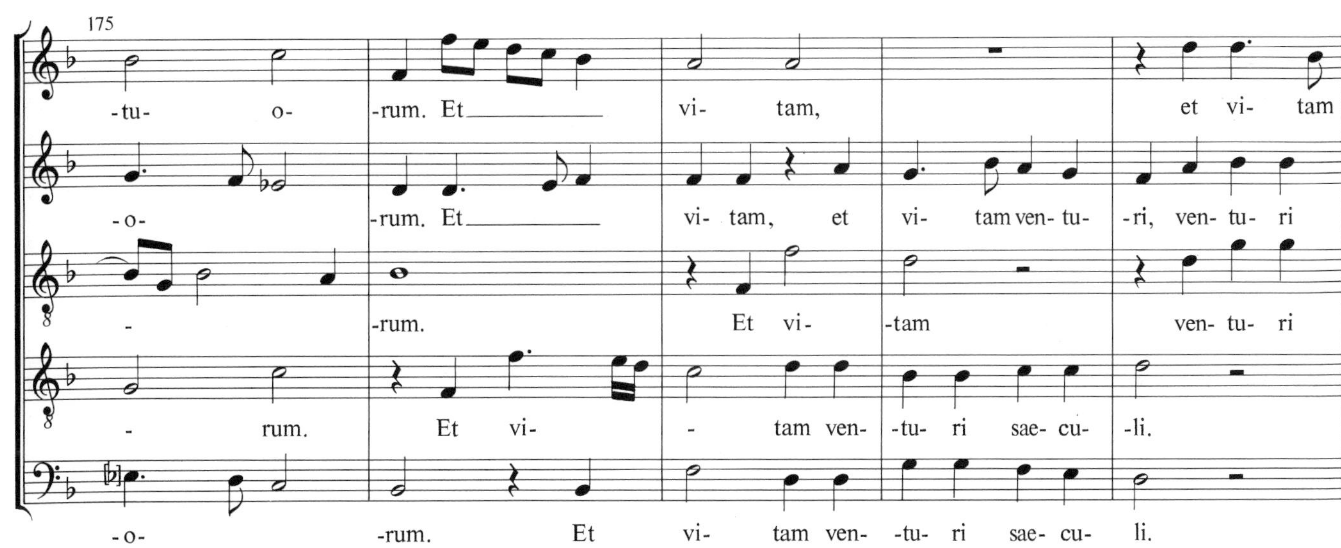
-tu- o- -rum. Et vi- tam, et vi- tam
-o- -rum. Et vi- tam, et vi- tam ven- tu- -ri, ven- tu- ri
- -rum. Et vi- -tam ven- tu- ri
- rum. Et vi- - tam ven- -tu- ri sae- cu- -li.
-o- -rum. Et vi- tam ven- -tu- ri sae- cu- li.

ven- tu- ri sae- - - cu- li.
sae- cu- li. A- - -men, A- -men,
sae- cu- li. A- - - -
A- -men, A- -
A- - men, [A-

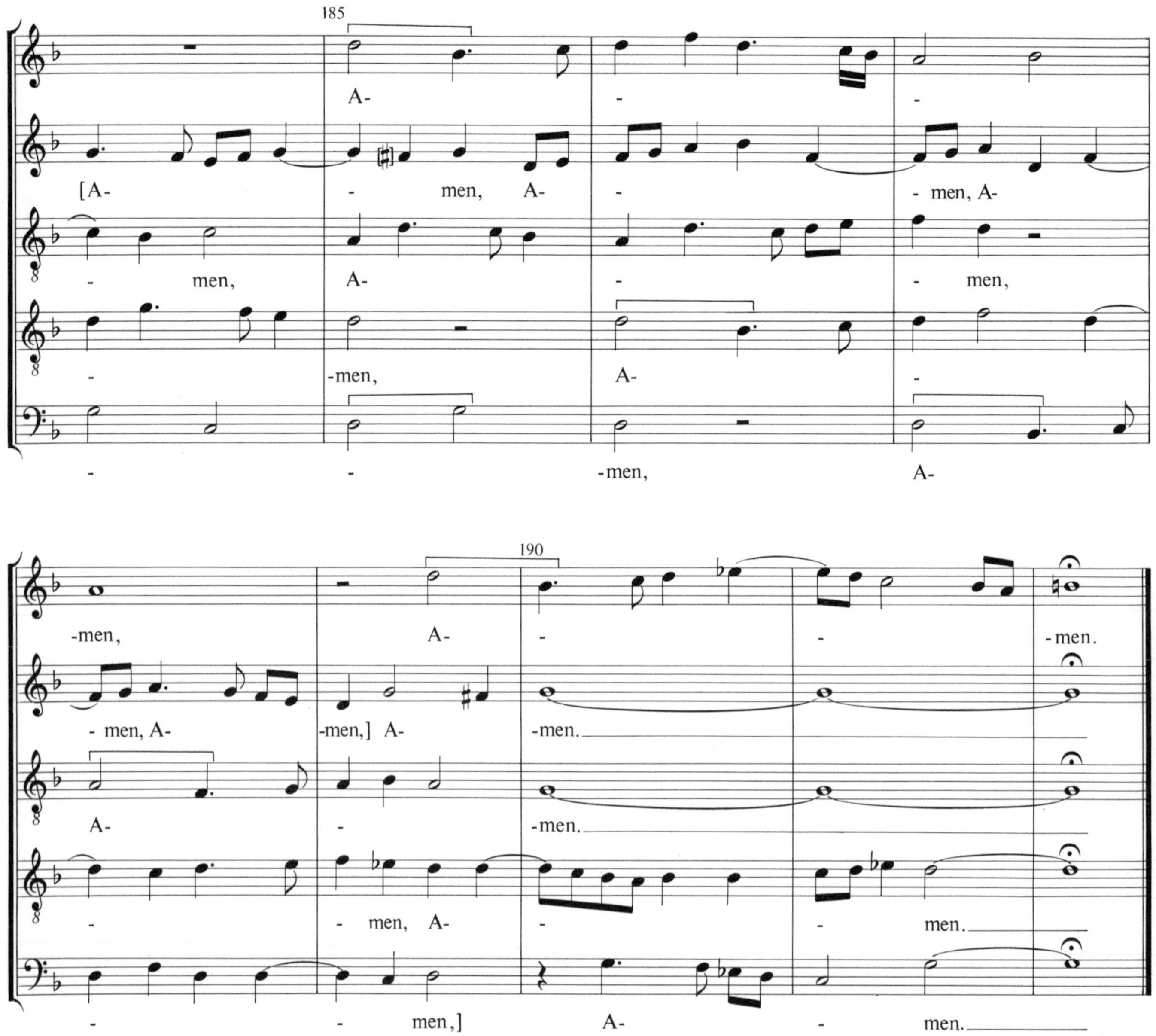

185
A- - -
[A- - men, A- - - men, A-
- men, A- - - men,
- -men, A- -
- - -men, A-
190
-men, A- - - -men.
- men, A- -men,] A- -men.
A- - -men.
- - men, A- - - men.
- - men,] A- - men.

Sanctus

San- ctus, San- - - ctus, [San- - ctus, San-
San- - ctus,
San- - - ctus,
San-

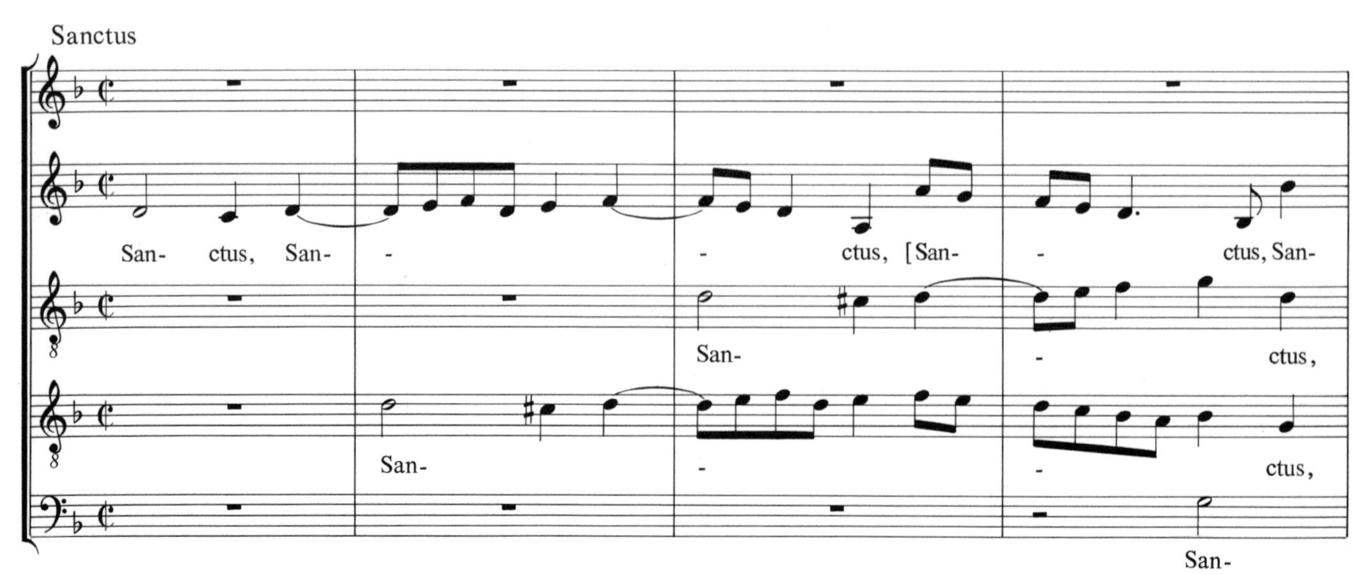

5
San- - -
- ctus, San- -ctus,] San- ctus Do-
San- ctus, San- - - ctus Do-mi-
[San- - ctus,] San- - ctus Do- mi- nus
-ctus, [San- -ctus,] San- - - ctus

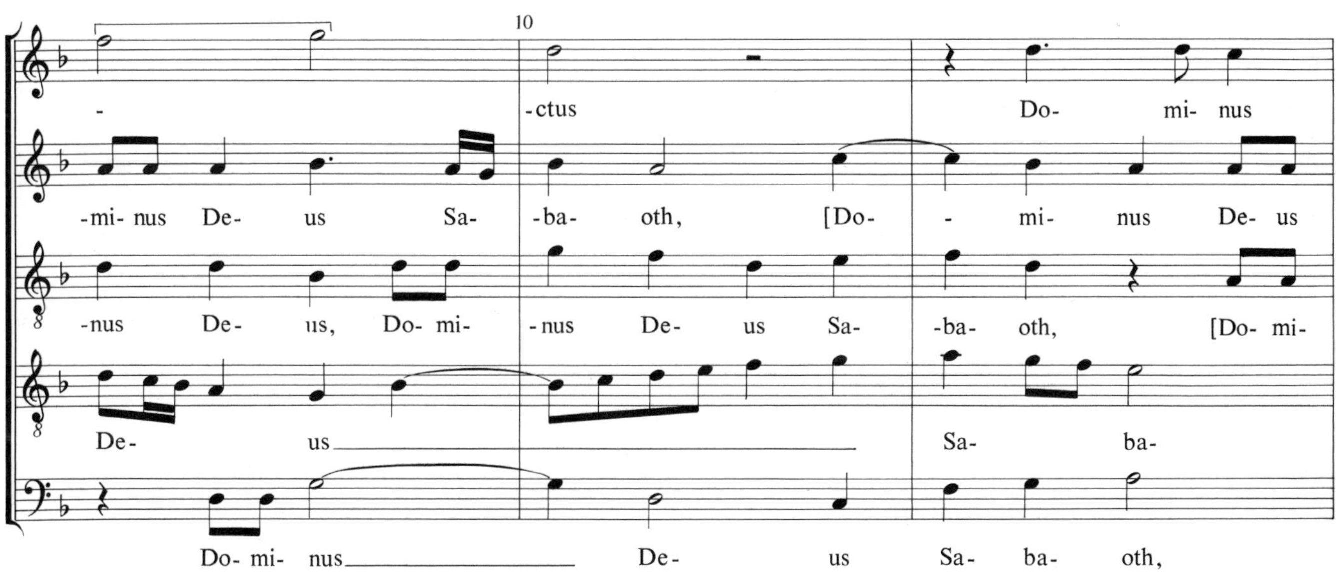
10
- -ctus Do- mi- nus
-mi- nus De- us Sa- -ba- oth, [Do- - mi- nus De- us
-nus De- us, Do- mi- -nus De- us Sa- -ba- oth, [Do- mi-
De- us Sa- ba-
Do- mi- nus De- us Sa- ba- oth,

15
De- us Sa- ba- -oth, [Do- -mi- nus De- us
Sa- ba- oth,] Do-mi- nus De- -us, Do- mi- nus De- - us.
-nus De- us,] Do- - mi- nus De- us Sa- ba- oth. Ple-
-oth, [Do-mi- -nus Sa- ba- oth, Do- -mi- nus Do- mi-
[Do-mi-nus De- - us Sa- ba- -oth.]

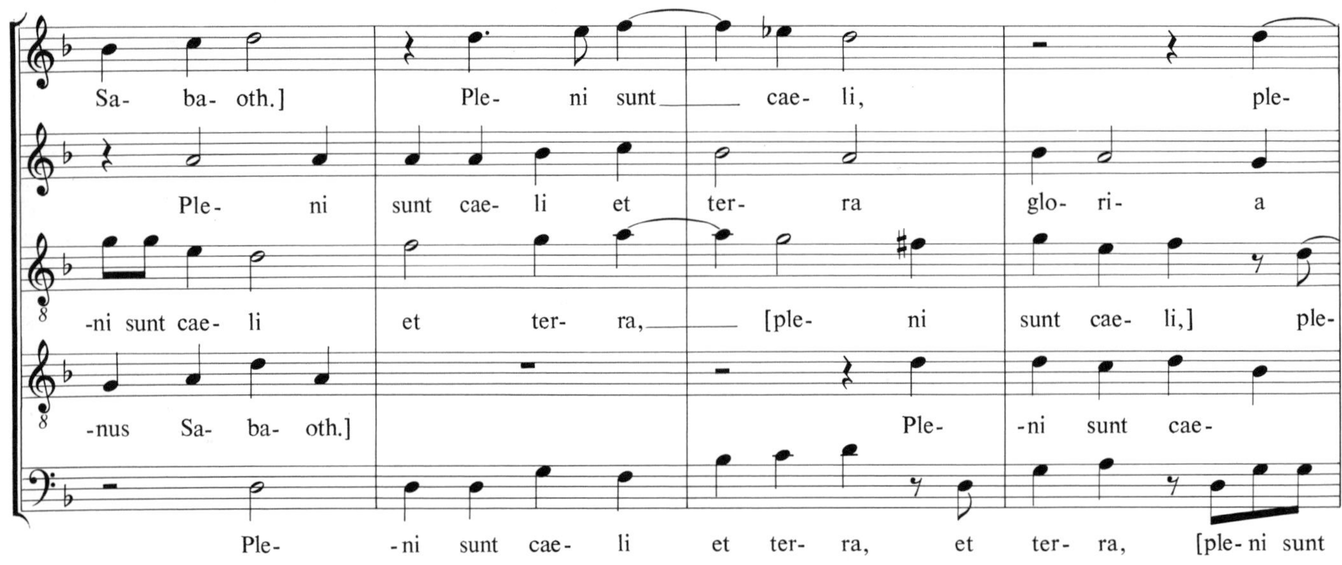
Sa- ba- oth.] Ple- ni sunt cae- li, ple-
Ple- ni sunt cae- li et ter- ra glo- ri- a
-ni sunt cae- li et ter- ra, [ple- ni sunt cae- li,] ple-
-nus Sa- ba- oth.] Ple- -ni sunt cae-
Ple- -ni sunt cae- li et ter- ra, et ter- ra, [ple- ni sunt

20
- ni sunt cae- li et ter- -ra, [ple- ni sunt cae- li et
tu- a, glo- -ri- a tu-
- ni sunt cae- li et ter- ra glo- ri- -a tu- a, [glo-
-li, ple- - ni sunt cae- li et ter- -
cae- li et ter- -ra, ple- -ni sunt cae- li

25
ter- ra] glo- -ri- a, glo- ri-
- a, [glo- -ri- a tu- a, glo- ri-
-ria tu- a, glo- - ri- -a tu- a,] glo- ri-
- ra, [ple- -ni sunt cae- li et ter- ra]
et ter- ra] glo- - ri- a tu- a,

30
-a tu- a, glo- ri- -a tu- a.
- a, glo- - ri- - a tu- -a.]
-a tu- a, [glo- -ri- a tu- a,] glo- ria tu- -a.
glo- ri- a tu- -a, tu- - a.
glo- ri- -a tu- - -a.

35
Be- -ne- di-
Be- - ne- di- ctus qui ve- nit, [be- - ne-di- ctus,
Be- ne- -di- ctus qui ve- nit, be-

-ctus qui ve- -nit, [be- - ne-di-ctus qui ve- -nit, be-ne- di-
] be- ne- - - di- -ctus,
Be- - ne- -di- ctus qui
- ne- di- - - ctus, [be- ne-

40
-ctus qui ve- -nit,] be- - ne- di- ctus qui ve-
be- -ne- di- -ctus qui ve- -nit
ve- nit, [be- ne- di- -ctus qui ve- -
-di- ctus,] be- -ne- di- ctus qui ve- - nit

45
-nit in no- mi- ne Do- mi- -ni, [in no- mi- ne,
in no- - mi- ne Do- - mi-
-nit] in no- mi- -ne Do- mi- ni, in no- mi-
in no- - mi- ne Do-mi- ni, [in

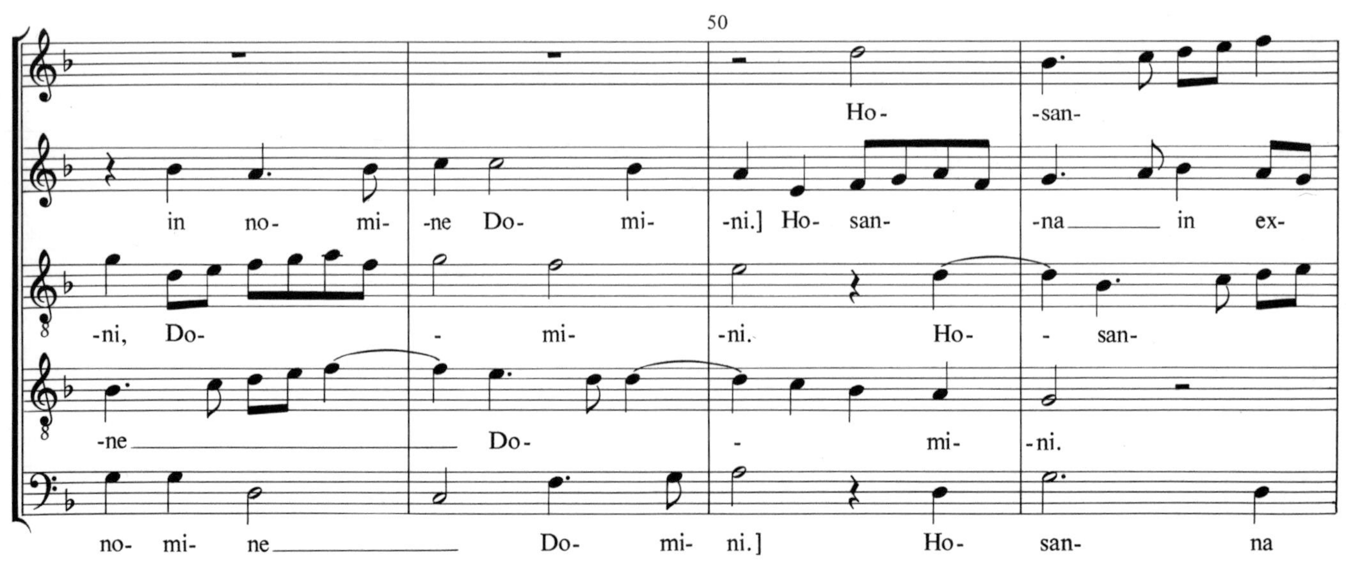
50
Ho- -san-
in no- mi- -ne Do- mi- -ni.] Ho- san- -na in ex-
-ni, Do- - mi- -ni. Ho- - san-
-ne Do- - mi- -ni.
no- mi- ne Do- mi- ni.] Ho- san- na

55
-na in ex- cel- sis, [ho- san- na in ex-
-cel- sis, [ho- -san- na in ex- cel- -sis, ho-
- na, ho- san- - na in ex- cel- sis,
Ho- san- na in ex- cel- sis, ho- -
in ex- - cel- sis ho- san-

-cel- sis,] [in ex- cel- - sis,] ho-
-san- na in ex- cel- - sis,] ho- san- - na in ex-
[in ex- cel- - -sis,] ho- -san-
-san- na in ex- cel- sis, ho- - san- - na in ex-
-na in ex- cel- sis, ho- - san-

60
-san- - na, ho- - san- na in ex- cel- -sis.
-cel- sis, [ho- -san- -na in ex- cel- - -sis.]
-na in ex- cel- - -sis.
-cel- sis, [ho- -san- -na in ex-cel- -sis.]
-na in ex- -cel- - -sis.

Agnus Dei

A- -gnus De- - -i,
A- - gnus De- - i, [A- - gnus
A- - gnus
A- - gnus De- -i, A- -

5
[A- gnus De- -i,] A- gnus De-
De- - i,] qui tol- lis
De- i, [A- - gnus De- -i,] A-
-gnus De- -i, [A- gnus De- -
A- - gnus De-

10
- i,
pec- ca- ta mun- -di, mun- di, [qui tol- lis pec-
-gnus De- - - -
-i,] A- - - gnus De-
-i, A- gnus De- - i,

15
qui tol- lis pe- ca- ta mun- -di, [qui tol- lis pec- ca-
-ca- ta mun- di, qui tol- lis pec- ca- ta
-i, qui tol- lis pec- ca- - ta mun- di, qui
-i, qui tol- -lis, qui tol- lis
qui tol- lis, qui tol- lis pec- ca- ta mun- -di,

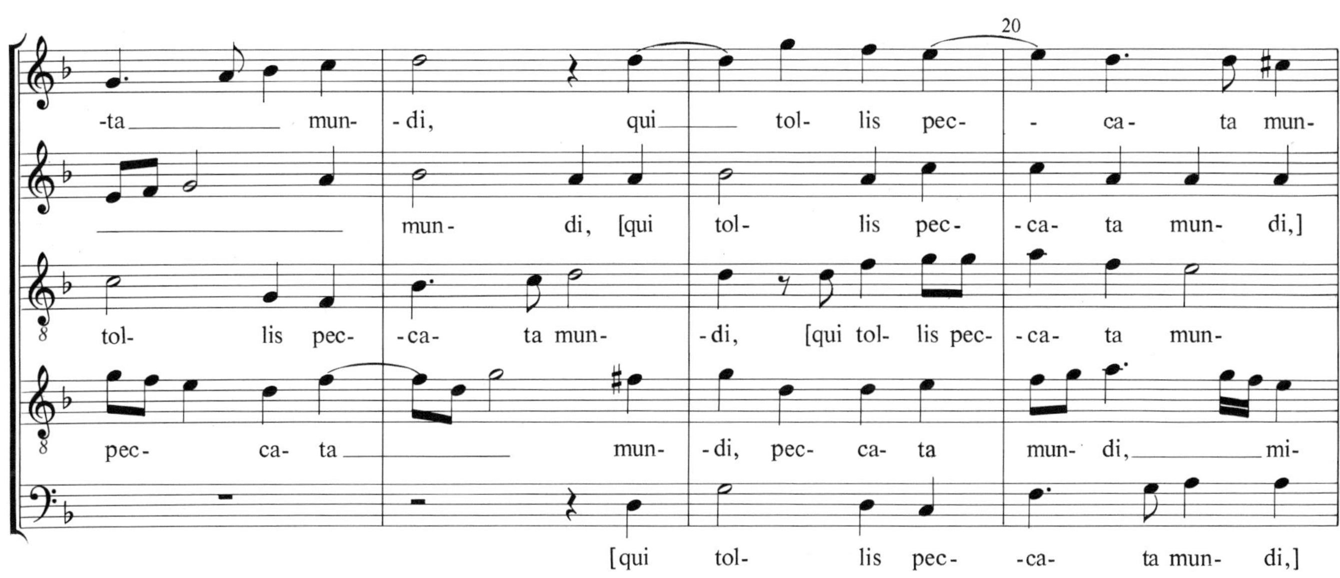
20
-ta mun- - di, qui tol- lis pec- - ca- ta mun-
mun- di, [qui tol- lis pec- -ca- ta mun- di,]
tol- lis pec- -ca- ta mun- -di, [qui tol- lis pec- -ca- ta mun-
pec- ca- ta mun- -di, pec- ca- ta mun- di, mi-
[qui tol- lis pec- -ca- ta mun- di,]

-di,] mi- se- re- - re no- -bis, [mi- se- -re- re no- bis,
mi- se- re- re no- bis, [mi- se- -re re no- bis,
-di,] mi- se- re- - re no- bis, [mi-
-se- re- re no- -bis, mi- se- re- - re no- bis, mi-
mi- se- re- re no- bis, [mi-

25
—] mi- se- -re- re no- bis, [mi- se-
mi- -se- re- re no- -bis, mi- se- re- -re no- bis,]
-se- re- re no- -bis, mi- se- re- -re no- bis,]
-se- re- re no- -bis, mi- se- re- re no- -bis, mi- se- re- re no- -bis, mi- se-
-se- re- re no- - bis,] mi- se- re- re, mi- se- re- re

30
-re- re,] mi- -se- re- -re, mi- se- re- -re no- -bis.
mi- se- re- -re no- -bis.
mi- se- -re- re no- -bis.
-re- re no- bis, mi- se- -re- re no- - -bis.
no- -bis, mi- se- -re- re no- -bis.